ANNE McCAFFREY

Starmont Reader's Guide 30

MARY T. BRIZZI

Series Editor: Roger C. Schlobin

Starmont House
Mercer Island, Washington
1986

Library of Congress Cataloging-in-Publication Data

Brizzi, Mary T.
   Anne McCaffrey.

   (Starmont reader's guide; 30)
   Bibliography: p.
   Includes index.
   1. McCaffrey, Anne – Criticism and interpretation.
I. Title.   II. Series.
PS 3563.A255Z59   1986   813'.54   85-17160
ISBN 0-930261-30-5
ISBN 0-930261-29-1 (pbk.)

Published and copyright ©1986 by Starmont House Inc., P. O. Box 851,
Mercer Island, WA 98040, USA.
Cover design by Stephen E. Fabian.

DR. MARY T. BRIZZI is an Associate Professor of English at the Trum-
bull Campus of Kent State University. She is a graduate of Clarion Writers
Workshop and Associate Editor of *Extrapolation*. She has published a
large variety of poems, reviews, and articles, as well as the *Reader's Guide
to Philip José Farmer.*

For
LEE RALPH TURZILLO
and
LUCILLE PELTIER TURZILLO

CONTENTS

TABLE OF ABBREVIATIONS FOR IN-TEXT CITATION

CANON AND CHRONOLOGY

1926	Born April 1, Cambridge, Massachusetts, to George H. McCaffrey and Anne D. McCaffrey (née McElroy).
1947	B.A., *cum laude,* Radcliffe College.
1950	Marries H. Wright Johnson.
1952	Son, Alec Johnson, born.
1953	"Freedom of the Race," first published science-fiction story.
1956	Son, Todd Johnson, born.
c. 1958–1965	Active in dramatic arts; participated in over 30 productions.
1959	"The Lady in the Tower," first acknowledged science-fiction publication. Daughter, Georgeanne, born.
1967	*Restoree,* "Weyr Search," "Dragonrider," Part I.
1968	"Dragonrider," Part II; *Dragonflight.* Awarded Hugo for "Weyr Search." Awarded Nebula for "Dragonrider."
1969	*Decision at Doona, The Ship Who Sang.*
1968–1970	Secretary to Science Fiction Writers of America.
1970	Edited *Alchemy and Academe.* Divorce. Move to Ireland.
1971	*Dragonquest, The Mark of Merlin, Ring of Fear.*
1973	*To Ride Pegasus, Cooking Out of this World.*
1975	*The Kilternan Legacy, A Time When.*
1976	*Dragonsong.* Awarded E. E. Smith Memorial Award for Imaginative Fiction ("Doc Smith" or Skylark).
1977	*Dragonsinger, Get Off the Unicorn.*
1978	*Dinosaur Planet, The White Dragon.*
1979	*Dragondrums.* Awarded Gandalf for *The White Dragon.*
1980	Awarded Balrogs for *Dragondrums* and Outstanding Professional Achievement.
1982	*The Crystal Singer.*
1983	*The Coelura, Moreta: Dragonlady of Pern.*
1984	*Dinosaur Planet Survivors.*

I
ANNE McCAFFREY'S LIFE, ACHIEVEMENT, AND THEMES

In 1968, Anne Inez McCaffrey broke ground by being the first woman ever to win the Hugo Award. A year later, she was the first female Nebula winner. Since then, she has won many other awards, most notably the E. E. Smith Memorial Award for Imaginative Fiction (also called the Skylark or "Doc Smith") in 1976 and the 1980 Balrog Award for Fantasy, Best Novel, and Outstanding Achievement. Her dragon books frequently constitute the first science fiction of young readers, as well as being the favorites of older readers who understand much that the younger audience misses. So popular are her dragon books that they have been translated into nine languages. She has spoken at scores of conventions, including the young adult section of the American Library Association, and Milwaukee Con, Balticon, Nova Con, Other Con, Tor Con, and many other science-fiction conventions, at which she has frequently been guest of honor. Her work—mostly the dragon books, but her other fiction too—has inspired a stream of sometimes almost hysterical fan material, including *Pern Portfolio*, a hundred-page compilation of derivative creative work and commentary, and *Crystal Singer*, a serial fanzine devoted to her. Other fanzines have devoted whole issues to her work, and there is an elaborate guild devoted to recreating Pernese society, rivaling the Society for Creative Anachronism in complexity: members advertise in *Crystal Singer* for fire-lizard eggs and hold allegiance to one or another weyr. There is a role-playing game, "Dragonriders of Pern," published by Mayfair Games of Chicago, in which players, using a map created by Tim Hildebrandt, solve strategic problems. McCaffrey has signed a movie contract for *Dragonflight* and will do the scripting for it. Music, records, tapes, and other peripheral material celebrate the popularity of McCaffrey's special planet where green-blooded, two-hearted, telepathic beasts defend mankind against Thread.

McCaffrey has published, at this writing, eighteen full-length science-fiction books, plus three gothic mysteries, an anthology, a science-fiction cookbook, and a body of short fiction and significant criticism in the field. She is a member of Science Fiction Writers of America, of which she was secretary-treasurer for 1968–1970; Author's Guild; P. E. N.; Mystery Writers of America; and the English Milford Society, of which she was co-founder and chairman for 1971–1975.

This remarkable woman is the product of an intellectually rich background. She was born April 1, 1926, in Cambridge, Massachusetts. Her mother, Anne Dorothy McCaffrey (née McElroy), to whom *Dragonquest* is dedicated, was a talented career woman whose writing ability served her as copywriter, ad writer, and real estate agent. In addition to these activities and raising Anne and two other children, this enterprising woman wrote mysteries, although none were ever published.

McCaffrey's father, George Herbert McCaffrey, was likewise a brilliant and forceful personality. Holder of a doctorate, he was chief political advisor to General Mark Clark, a military governor of several provinces in Italy during World War II, where a bridge in Palermo is named for him, and a tax advisor in occupied Japan and in Pusan, Korea. Colonel Sartorius in *A Bell for Adano*, by John Hersey, is supposed to be modeled after George McCaffrey. At his death in 1954, his obituary occupied a twelve-inch column in the *New York Times*. He is the author of *Metropolitan Boston*.

McCaffrey also had two brothers, Hugh and Kevin, who influenced her early life, and a favorite aunt, G. N. McElroy, to whom she dedicated *Restoree*. Significantly, Anne McCaffrey's mother, father, older brother Hugh, and three nieces all have been writers, and her son Todd has collaborated with her. The early influence of this inventive and cultured family may well have created for McCaffrey both the high ideals and personal warmth that she depicts in scenes of family life in her own fiction.

A self-directed learner, McCaffrey sought and found high-quality educational opportunities in Upper Montclair, New Jersey, to develop her complex and varied talents as she grew up. She began writing in earnest at age eight, hunting and pecking on a family typewriter to compose. At Girl Scout camp, she wrote, produced, directed, and starred in a fantasy-oriented play.[1] When study of Latin in junior high school failed to galvanize her attention, she penned a 20,000-word novel called *Eleutheria, the Dancing Slave* during class time. In spite of her inattention to class activities, she still knows enough Latin to throw an occasional phrase into speeches and essays. Shortly afterward, she wrote a western novel, titled *Flame, Chief of Herd and Track*, evincing an early interest in horses that later emerged in her gothic mysteries and in the symbolism of her science fiction. Neither novel has been published.

Early literary influences on McCaffrey were O. Henry and Saki (from whom she learned economical and effective plotting as well as poker-faced irony), A. Merritt (about whom she learned from her mother), Edgar Rice Burroughs (both the Tarzan and the John Carter books), Anthony Hope, and Rudyard Kipling. Her favorite book is Austin Tappan Wright's *Islandia*.

Though her interest turned to dramatics and music (she has studied voice for nine years, an interest evident in such works as *Dragonsong, Dragonsinger, Dragondrums, The Ship Who Sang*, and *The Crystal Singer*), her major at Radcliffe was Slavic languages and literature, where she made the dean's list and graduated *cum laude*. Her senior thesis compared Zamyatin's *We* to Aldous Huxley's *Brave New World*. She has studied ten

4

languages, including Russian, Polish, Czech, French, Old Irish, German, Latin, and Spanish, though she modestly claims that now she can only swear in them. McCaffrey's science background comes from reading, postgraduate courses, tutoring, personal conferences with scientists, and such diverse printed sources as Isaac Asimov's science popularizations and the Merck Manual.[2] Since McCaffrey's training in science has not been under university auspices, she tends to be rather apologetic about it; however, she is extremely meticulous about every phase of technology in her work. Critics who take the trouble to research casual details in her ecologies, astronomy, etc., are often amazed to find that her work is remarkably current, accurate, detailed, and advanced. *Dinosaur Planet* presents a particular challenge to the amateur scientist.

McCaffrey's public creative career began in music rather than writing. An innovator in musical tent theater, she performed in or directed over thirty productions with the Wilmington Opera Society, the Brecks Mill Cronies, and elsewhere. Her roles ranged from the Old Woman in *Candide* to Queen Agravane in *Once Upon a Mattress,* including performances in such widely varying works as *Kiss Me, Kate, The Devil and Daniel Webster, Amahl and the Night Visitors, Hansel and Gretel, Down in the Valley, The Merry Widow, The Vagabond King, Die Fledermaus,* and *Babes in Arms.* As the climax of her musical and dramatic career, she directed and performed in the American premiere of *Ludus de Nato Infante Mirificus,* by Carl Orff, at the University of Delaware. One of the musicians with whom she worked, Frederick N. Robinson of Pennsylvania's Lancaster Opera Workshop, became the model for Master Robinton, the kindly and visionary master musician of Pern. McCaffrey is also collaborating with Jon Anderson of the contemporary music group Yes on a musical interpretation of *Dragonflight.* She was active in music and theater from about 1958 to 1965.

After her graduation in 1947 from Radcliffe, McCaffrey held several positions that made use of her ability with languages and writing. She worked with World Trade Intelligence, Friedman Diecutters, Pongee Corporation, Liberty Music Shops, and Helena Rubenstein.

McCaffrey married H. Wright Johnson, a Princeton graduate, in June 1950. Although Johnson never particularly encouraged her science-fiction writing, he did share her musical activities and had a pleasing bass voice. The couple had three children: Alec, born in 1952; Todd, born in 1956; and Georgeanne ("Gi Gi"), born in 1959. The couple divorced in 1970, and McCaffrey moved to Ireland with her mother and the two younger children. As she had kept her maiden name in science-fiction writing, she was amused to confound friends of her middle child by inscribing *Decision at Doona,* which is dedicated to Todd Johnson, "Yes, he *is* my son." McCaffrey's family orientation and keen insight into child and adolescent psychology is evident throughout her work.

McCaffrey's interest in science fiction may have been stimulated by her early reading in dystopian and utopian works, such as Zamyatin's *We* and Wright's *Islandia,* but her notion of actually writing science fiction began when she found an abandoned cache of it in an apartment she had just moved into. Among her early favorites at this stage was Edmund Hamilton's *The Star Kings.*

Her initial publication was a story in *Science-Fiction Plus* of October 1953, "Freedom of the Race." This rather lurid but economically written short-short story contained ideas that McCaffrey was to develop in the next thirty years: human-alien interaction, alien reproduction, and the theme of feminine courage. In the story, alien imperialists implant their own young into the womb of Terran women. But nurses of the involuntary human hosts sabotage the births by exposing the human mother and alien fetus to German measles. McCaffrey does not like this story today and prefers to recognize "The Lady in the Tower" as her first publication. It is not clear why she rejects her first story; perhaps too many questions about the compatibility of alien and human physiology are left unanswered. Perhaps the grisly pessimism of the premise—biological warfare—repels her. However, the pacing and plotting show excellent control over the short-short form, the language is economical and vivid, and the situation is tense and suspenseful. It is clearly the work of a promising young writer.

McCaffrey later developed some of the technical ideas in later work. The idea of inovulation is followed up in "The Greatest Love" (1977), and the horrible punishment devised by the aliens for uncooperative host-mothers, called slow-burn, is a precursor to the Thread of the Dragon books, a mycorrhyzoid organism that also attacks flesh and eats its way through.

The years from the publication of this story to the appearance of "The Lady in the Tower" (*F&SF*, April 1959) were busy ones for McCaffrey, filled with two more births and the raising of three children. The family moved to Wilmington, Delaware, where McCaffrey's husband worked for Dupont. McCaffrey herself filled her days with more than childrearing and homemaking; during this period, she was also active in musical theater. But her drive to write and publish continued, and so she was flattered when Algis Budrys and Bob Mills liked one of her stories enough to help her revise and publish it. So pleased was she with the result that she prefers to think of this story as her first "acknowledged" publication. "The Lady in the Tower" and its sequel, "A Meeting of Minds," feature powerful female psi talents working in synergy with machines. McCaffrey originally intended to incorporate them into a novel called *The Bitter Tower.* Both have an unabashed "romance and glamour" angle and depict women as powerful and significant people who nonetheless cannot achieve their full potential without sympathetic male support —ideas that continue to inform McCaffrey's work.

The strong, romantic female protagonist continued to develop in McCaffrey's work in the sixties. She wrote and published "The Ship Who Sang," "The Ship Who Mourned," "The Ship Who Killed," "The Ship Who Disappeared," and "Dramatic Mission," all of which were incorporated into the novel *The Ship Who Sang* (1969). Helva, the heroine, represents the multifaceted feminine personality in McCaffrey's work— capable of love, art, work, and, if necessary, killing. *Restoree* (1967),

6

McCaffrey's mock gothic with a science-fiction twist, and *Decision at Doona* (1970), a story with strong family interest that emphasizes the importance of individuality in children, were also products of this period. McCaffrey produced a number of short pieces, too, including several of the pieces on psi talent that later comprised *To Ride Pegasus* (1973). Most significant of these was her 1969 "A Womanly Talent," the first story with an explicit sex scene ever published in *Analog.* But the triumph of the sixties were "Weyr Search" (*Analog,* October 1967) and "Dragonrider" (*Analog,* December 1967 and January 1968), the respective winners of the Hugo and Nebula Awards. *Dragonflight,* of which these stories are part, is the basis of all the Pern fiction, probably McCaffrey's biggest money-maker, and the basis of the fame that eventually permitted her to support herself and her family as a career science-fiction writer. Appropriately, her home in Ireland is called Dragonhold for the concept that financed it. And in the long run, the dragon books will remain the foundation of McCaffrey's reputation as a writer.

The triumphs of the sixties did not end McCaffrey's struggles to earn a living as a science-fiction writer. Her divorce in 1970 and subsequent setbacks in her ex-husband's finances taxed her resources. She points with pride to her ability to finance her children's education and to maintain a good standard of living in Ireland. The move to Ireland, in 1970, was influenced by a number of factors: pride in her Irish heritage, economics, violence in her daughter's school. But the move created some problems: financing a home for an "unemployed" divorcee was not easy in tradition-minded Ireland. McCaffrey demonstrates a touch of pride as she tells of showing mortgage agents her book contracts to demonstrate her prospects for making mortgage payments. And, though McCaffrey was able to study meteorology at the University of Dublin, her early years in Ireland were saddened by the death of her mother, who had made the move with her.

Dragonhold itself is conventional in appearance by American standards, but a center of friendship and humanitarian works, as well as creativity. McCaffrey and her friends are active in animal rescue, for mistreatment of animals is repugnant to McCaffrey, who like so many of her heroines is strongly empathic to animals. She is remarkably accessible to fans, answering letters and making herself available for interviews. During my visit to her, when I gathered much of the information for this chapter, she casually spoke of the arrival and departure of several guests. Her living room is decorated with draconica, including a Colin Saxton rendering that she considers nearest her mental picture of dragons.

McCaffrey makes a vivid personal impression. As mentioned in all personal sketches, she has green eyes. She also has abundant white hair and a very lively, mobile face. When I met her in her home, she was wearing blue jeans (which, she mentioned, could have been her son's) and a sweater, with penny loafers. However, she is fond of elegant clothing and at public appearances wears stunning outfits. She is known for wearing a red-lined black cloak to conventions. An engaging conversationalist, she often reveals a mind three steps ahead of her interlocutor. Her humor is subtle, which is why some of her irony in writing is missed by readers. She

7

is extremely energetic and travels extensively to make appearances at conventions in the United States and elsewhere.

Her personal interests are varied. Besides owning a variety of dogs, cats, and sometimes a horse or two, she cooks, designs clothing, and knits Aran sweaters worthy of praise from the local Irish. She still sings and has been known to do duets with Isaac Asimov, who is a tenor. She is genuinely interested in the sciences, with particular fascination for geology, paleontology, meteorology, ecology, social systems, biology, and chemistry.

McCaffrey's strengths as a writer are primarily her inventiveness, her ability to detail worlds, her insight into the psychology of children, her portrayal of love relationships, her memorable female characters, and her symbolism. Her weakness, if she has one, is diction: Robert Silverberg has cautioned her against excess use of adverbs, and James Blish suggested avoiding synonyms for the word *said*.[3] Harlan Ellison objects to her occasional lapses into the language of gothic romance.[4] Ellison criticizes her portrayal of male characters, but diction is probably the real problem here. Certainly McCaffrey portrays a variety of believable, masculine men, from F'lar and F'nor to Robinton, not to speak of the profane Niall Parollan of *The Ship Who Sang*.

Another aspect of McCaffrey's style is her use of irony. Perhaps because she seldom uses a first-person narrator, her unreliable narrators are difficult to see through—perhaps too difficult for many readers.[5] Hence it is possible to misread radically *Restoree* as a serious romantic space opera, in spite of the patent absurdities of science, technology, and situation. In my chapter on *The Crystal Singer,* I argue that Killashandra's blindness to the evil around her creates ironic tension in the novel. Subtle irony is also used in McCaffrey's masterful short story, "A Proper Santa Claus," discussed in my chapter on *Get Off the Unicorn.*

McCaffrey's symbolism is subtle, rich, and yet exciting. She uses fairy tales, particularly the story of Cinderella, in many stories. Sara, in *Restoree,* is converted from a homely, big-nosed spinster to an exciting lovely girl dressed in rich robes. Menolly, in *Dragonsong,* goes from being a gawky, ill-treated bumpkin to being a respected musician. In *Dragonflight,* Lessa is dressed in rags when we first meet her; later she becomes the elegant rider of a golden dragon. McCaffrey even has a story called "Cinderella Switch."

McCaffrey uses mythology to underline some of her symbolism, though the mythological names are used very subtly. McCaffrey keeps lists of typographical errors and foreign words to use as futuristic or alien names; she seems to alter the names of Greek goddesses and heroes by only a few letters so that their symbolic function is less blatant. So with the names of Lessa, Jaxom, and B'lerion, as discussed in my chapter on the Pern novels.

McCaffrey's grounding in English and American literature also provides her with a wealth of material for symbolism. She quotes Shakespeare, Kipling, and Pope extensively and uses names from Shakespeare in *The Ship Who Sang* to complement the dramatic theme in the plot. Her use of Yeats in the Pern novels is very exciting, and I suspect, though I can't prove, that the words *Pass* and *Turn* in these novels are derived from Ralph Waldo Emerson's poem "Brahma."

The most pervasive symbol in McCaffrey's work is a metaphor for the imaginative faculty itself. I call this metaphor the *horse-and-rider motif,* though it takes many forms: ship and brain in *The Ship Who Sang*; Talent and pegasus in *To Ride Pegasus*; dragon and rider in *Dragonflight*; fire lizard and musician in *Dragonsong*; crystal and singer in *The Crystal Singer*. In each case, I will argue that the horse represents a vehicle, a talent that exalts the rider, the imaginative human being. By mounting the horse, the pegasus, or the dragon, the rider is taking a risky ride that will elevate his soul. The ride, whether it be horse-back, dragon-back, pegasus-back, perhaps even unicorn-back, is an imaginative leap that enobles and creates joy. The imaginative flight in the horse-and-rider motif is often an artistic flight, but it is more than artistic. By flying or riding thus—in a space ship or on a dragon, while fighting Thread or cutting crystal—the "rider" is lifted toward the absolute, transcending the mundane and approaching the Ideal.

In spite of the popularity of McCaffrey's works, there has been little attempt to place her as a literary figure. One point of view, represented by Rosemarie Arbur, is that McCaffrey's work has to be experienced on a purely visceral level, that criticism in terms of archetypes or symbols can only be reduced to absurdity.[6] The other major point of view, represented by Marleen Barr, is that McCaffrey is a feminist.[7] I do not think McCaffrey is a radical or traditional feminist, though there are strong feminist elements in her work and though feminists will always find authenticity there. Nor do I think McCaffrey's work is "silent" on a literary or symbolic level. Rather, I believe that McCaffrey's main themes, as an engaged artist, are first the creative process as a liberating force through art and second, the growth of creative energy through bonding. I further hold that these themes are expressed through spaceflight and dragonflight, through nervous connection of singer and singing material, through the joining of cyborg and machine.

We may justly expect from science-fiction criticism something partially different from what we expect from standard literary criticism—partially different, in that even the science-fiction critic should relate his work loosely to the body of criticism in general, though without the expectation that he shall use some extreme theory inappropriate for the science-fiction work. Marxist criticism may be more useful to science fiction than deconstructionism. But there is also the expectation that science-fiction criticism will touch matters of symbolism, form, structure, characterization, style, literary antecedents, narrative voice, etc. In two regards, the science-fiction critic will meet slightly different expectations: first, she will make some attempt to justify considering the works and author in question as serious literary phenomena. Why, she will ask (and answer), is Anne McCaffrey worthy of treatment as a writer of literature as opposed to a producer of mere entertainment? Second, the science-fiction critic will investigate the relationship of the works analyzed to science and technology as they are presently understood: in other words, to probability. The improbable but believable world is acceptable, but the improbable should not be stretched to the laughable. Moreover, attention to detail in shaping imaginary environments (Pern, Ireta, Doona, future Earth) will be considered evidence of literary merit. And not only will imagination and verisimilitude be praiseworthy, but their interrelationship —imagination working in concert with scientific detail, what the science-fiction critic calls *extrapolation*—is the highest goal to which good science fiction can aspire. This is what good science fiction does best. To the degree that imagination and scientific detail harmonize in an elaborate and interesting way, we say the writer achieves the sense of wonder.

How do these general demands we make upon science fiction and upon science-fiction criticism apply to Anne McCaffrey and to this book? The issues I will treat, with respect to individual works, are these:

1. To what extent does McCaffrey use the elements of literature skill-fully and artistically? Is she more than an artisan? Do her themes have significance?

2. With what ingenuity does McCaffrey use source material, whether her source be musicology, stellar evolution, ecology, or whatever?

3. To what extent does McCaffrey extrapolate skillfully and artisti-cally? Does she use scientific information of sufficient depth and novelty to produce the sense of wonder? Does she extrapolate with ingenuity? Are her extrapolated worlds novel and interesting? Are they in accord with present-day scientific knowledge?

I will maintain in this study, as I believe true in science fiction generally, that the inventions of science fiction writers are a metaphor for the crea-tive process. Further, these inventions stir the creative and imaginative faculty in the reader, so that the metaphor is extended to that reader, making the process of reading an active, not merely passive, process. Finally, this lively and intensely arousing transaction by which the creative process is at once described and evoked is properly called the sense of wonder. This is McCaffrey's achievement.

I express my thanks for information and assistance to the following people: Virginia Roos, David McClintock, Tess Kolney, Anne Zeek, Betsy Hoobler, Carl Yoke, Roger Schlobin, Bill Bowers, Rosemarie Arbur, Mike Gustovich, Betty Hall, Barbara Savage, Sam Benigni, Don Rayl, Grant Barkley, Fred Ineman, Ed Harrison, P. K. Saha, Jack Brizzi Sr., Jack Brizzi Jr., Virginia Schultz, Jerry Aurand, Jane Turzillo, Judith McCarron, Bonita Stoufer, Jerome Stephens, Evelina Smith, Debbie Murphy, Jay Molendyke, Rose Clark, Barbara Bell, Doris Mehegan, David Aylward, John Dunham, Virginia Kidd, Judy-Lynn del Rey, Harlan Ellison, and the wizard of word processing, Vicki Marcink. My thanks also to Anne McCaf-frey herself for her cooperation.

NOTES

[1] Ed Naha, "Living with Dragons: Anne McCaffrey," *Future*, No. 6 (November 1978), pp. 22–23, 74.

[2] For a description of her research methods, see "The Unscientific Approach to

Science Fiction: A Speech by Anne McCaffrey," *Luna'*, No. 8 (1970), pp. 3-9.

[3] Naha, 23.

[4] Harlan Ellison, "A Voice from the Styx," in *The Book of Ellison,* ed. Andrew Porter (New York: Algol, 1978), pp. 133, 137.

[5] I am using the term *unreliable narrator* loosely to cover the many types of narrative irony described in Wayne C. Booth's *The Rhetoric of Fiction* (Chicago: University of Chicago Press, 1961).

[6] Rosemarie Arbur, *Leigh Brackett, Marion Zimmer Bradley, Anne McCaffrey: A Primary and Secondary Bibliography* (Boston: G. K. Hall, 1982), p. xxi.

[7] Marleen Barr, "Science Fiction and the Fact of Women's Repressed Creativity: Anne McCaffrey Portrays a Female Artist," *Extrapolation,* 23, No. 1 (Spring 1982), 70-76.

II
RESTOREE AND *DECISION AT DOONA*
Two Novels of Exploration, Imagination, and Daring

Restoree (1967) and *Decision at Doona* (1969) are appropriate to study together because they both depict humans evolving a coequal relationship with an alien species. In each, a vulnerable but charming protagonist is accidentally cast in the role of first contact and goodwill ambassador. In *Restoree,* Sara Fulton is scooped up by a ship of alien cannibals and deposited on a world of humanoid aliens where she forms a pair-bond by becoming lovers with one alien. In *Decision at Doona,* the vulnerable human ambassador is a little boy, Todd Reeve, part of a colonial team which was not intended to encounter alien sentients. He forms a different type of pair-bond, a boyhood friendship, with a catlike alien "cub," Hrriss. Both Sara and Todd prove very good at alien language and protocol and ultimately are drafted to help cement friendly relations between humans and aliens. Traditionally in science fiction, the role of first contact is assigned to a macho spaceman; McCaffrey's more sensitive and egalitarian treatment of this theme uses a woman and a child in the explorer-ambassador role.

Another reason to study *Restoree* and *Decision at Doona* together is that both represent work of the late 1960s when McCaffrey was experimenting with form. Science fiction tends to be conservative in formal experimentation because idea content often makes it difficult enough to understand even *without* parodic elements or trick narrators. Yet, in these two novels, McCaffrey does experiment. In *Restoree,* she parodies the gothic and space-opera form; in *Decision at Doona,* she uses misleading narrative in early chapters to create later plot surprises.

When Virginia Kidd first took Anne McCaffrey on as a literary agency client, the skeptic might have said she was taking a long shot. McCaffrey had published a few stories about Helva and about Talent, and these showed a fresh viewpoint and fine storytelling ability. The first McCaffrey novel that Kidd took on to sell, however, was one of a kind. Critics still argue about whether its space-opera/gothic-romance premise is a parody or a relentlessly honest appeal to the primitive romanticism in every woman's—and many men's—atavistic subconscious mind. One thing is certain—*Restoree* is like no other science-fiction novel ever published.

The basic story is rich in invention and plot intricacies. Sara Fulton, an ugly New England girl, is kidnapped by the Mil, unicellular, evil-smelling aliens who have a perverse taste for sentient meat. The Mil proceed to flay

Sara, but an alien physician, Monsorlit from the planet Lothar, grafts onto her body a new, pretty, alien skin, not realizing that she is of a race Lotharians have previously not encountered. She is drafted into being a nursemaid for Harlan, a Lotharian nobleman whom Monsorlit's evil bosses drug to keep out of politics. Emerging from shock, she withholds the drug from Harlan, and the two escape. Harlan falls in love with her, and the pair, embroiled in Machiavellian politics, help instate Harlan's nephew Maxil as Warlord and defeat the Mil. Through all of this, Sara has to keep her identity secret because the skin-graft operation she underwent makes her a restoree—hence the title. Restoration is illegal because the restoree has, in the past, always turned out to be a zombie. In fact, restorees, like the surgeons who restore them, are subject to capital punishment.

McCaffrey herself calls *Restoree* a "tongue-in-cheek protest, utilizing as many of the standard 'thud and blunder' cliches as possible with one new twist—the heroine was the viewpoint character and *she* was always Johanna-on-the-spot."[1] She refers to the book as a "parody"; to critics who took the book seriously, she says, "You *clownheads* . . . I'm *teasing* you!"[2] Whatever the intent of the book, it does use the standard cliche of alien monsters threatening a woman, and McCaffrey does reverse roles by allowing Sara to be instrumental in defeating the alien monsters. It is true Sara does not invent the sonic vibrations that kill the Mil, nor does she join in the space-battle against them. But she is unique in not succumbing to mind-destroying fear on the Mil—almost emblematic of a feminist self-assertion *not* to be a helpless, hapless, stereotyped excuse for a character anymore. As to parody, there are some strikingly odd inconsistencies in Lotharian culture, as the existence of telecommunications and force fields without electricity (*R* 37, 190), the sacredness of potential mothers in spite of overpopulation (*R* 33, 53), and no organized religion, but an established priesthood (*R* 91, 122). The science in the novel and the technology of Lothar (*R* 67) are highly improbable, but planned with the aid of a research scientist.[3] Parodies are supposed to be not just incongruous but also funny, and while *Restoree* has its comic moments (Sara is concerned that she doesn't know the banalities of Lotharian existence, like "Joe Dimaggio, hot dogs, Fourth of July, and hammer murders" (*R* 90); the invisible iris-dilating wastebaskets (*R* 107) are amusing, too), it fails to exaggerate either science-fiction or gothic stereotypes far enough to qualify as true burlesque. Perhaps the true humor is evident only to the rare reader who is widely read in both genres. Or perhaps McCaffrey's humor, as elsewhere, is so subtle it escapes many readers.

It is possible to ignore the parodic intent of *Restoree* and view it seriously. Elsewhere, I argue that McCaffrey touches upon narcissistic archetypes drawn from fairy tales.[4] Certainly it follows the Cinderella pattern evident with other McCaffrey heroines. Sara is a homely household drudge, forced to wait on her insensitive brothers. She escapes to New York and undergoes a transformation at the hands of the Mil (who mutilate her) and Monsorlit (who makes her beautiful). Running with (rather than

13

from) her Prince Charming, Harlan, she loses her shoes (*R* 40); is lent a sumptuously beautiful gown; goes to a ball; later undergoes a recognition scene based not on foot size, but on the fact that she can't write; and ultimately marries her Prince Charming. The happily-ever-after is as vague in *Restoree* as in the fairy tale because Harlan simply assumes that Sara can bear his offspring (*R* 234).

Another fairy tale reflected in *Restoree* is the Ugly Duckling. Sara before her restoration is scarred, fat, hook-nosed, and hairy in all the wrong places. Her restoration cures all these afflictions. Less obviously, Harlan is an Ugly Duckling. At first she sees him as "an ugly man with vacant eyes . . . and sallow pitted skin" (*R* 7). Released from the poison, later, he is "no longer an ugly person" (*R* 24).

McCaffrey creates her own fairy tale in *Restoree* in the story of the Searcher and the Priest. The beautiful Searcher, in Lotharian folklore, goes about looking for her lover, who has been eaten by the Mil. The cannibalistic Mil are perfect fairy-tale creatures, a combination of Hansel and Gretel's witch, the big bad wolf, and Jack-in-the-Beanstalk's ogre. After a suitable period of wandering, however, the Searcher is claimed by a Priest. Apparently the priesthood of Lothar was originally linked to Mil-worship (*R* 28). That this rather cynical myth has popular appeal is incidentally illustrated by the fact that one of the winning costumes at the World Science Fiction Convention in 1982 was a richly clad Searcher and her Priest.

The allusiveness of *Restoree* is not exhausted with discussion of the fairy-tale elements, however. Sara herself is a creature of mythic significance. Sara in the Bible is a mother of nations, by being the wife of Abraham. Sara in *Restoree* will also have illustrious children (*R* 234). Sara Fulton of *Restoree* has a brother named Seth, one of Adam's sons. Her Adamic connotations are reinforced by her frequent eating of a Lotharian fruit that looks like an apple (*R* 83, 107, 117, for examples). She also has Christ-like qualities in that she "dies" in a Mil raid, harrows hell in a Mil ship, and is resurrected by Monsorlit. Through her ability to survive an experience that has killed all others who have undergone it, like Christ, she saves lives of future restorees. In addition, she brings scientific and technical information to Lothar—knowledge of a new world, plus paper and zippers. "Sara," says Harlan, "has a curious habit of supplying our need" (*R* 231).

Sara is also involved in McCaffrey's flight image that later develops into the horse-and-rider motif. Harlan assigns her a fictional birthplace in Jurasse, and the terrestrial Jurassic period is associated with the advent of birds. The Lotharians use aerial travel rather than roads; Sara makes numerous flights in aircars throughout the book and at one point refers to the other air traffic as "vultures and hummingbirds" (*R* 77). Her contact point after the Searcher charade is supposed to be the Place of Birds (*R* 52, 77). Fernan, the unpleasant young man who nearly becomes Warlord, is described as "canary-satiated" (*R* 101)—as if the protagonists of the novel were birds, subject to Fernan's cat-like preying. And the Glan, aliens allied with Lothar against the Mil, are "willowy skeletons with three

14

digits and an opposing thumb . . . covered with a fine down . . . their faces, long and narrow" (*R* 175)—as if evolved from a primitive bird-race.

Though McCaffrey's avowed aim in *Restoree* is not the creation of realistic or deep characters, Harlan, Sara, Maxil, and Monsorlit represent types that she develops in future novels. Like F'lar of the dragon series, Harlan tends to shake his lady to get her complete attention (*R* 163, 177, 178, 223). His ability to take risks and, more important, to cast his woman in important risk-taking roles is also a characteristic he shares with F'lar. Sara's ingenuity in getting out of predicaments prefigures the inventiveness of Lessa, Menolly, Helva, Killashandra, and others. McCaffrey's women characters are seldom at a loss for a plan. Maxil prefigures some of McCaffrey's adolescent males in later works, notably Jaxom, whose romantic troubles parallel Maxil's. The most interesting character in *Restoree* is Monsorlit, the brilliant, enigmatic, Svengali-like scientist. Monsorlit almost seems an early study for Lanzecki of *The Crystal Singer*.

First novels, in science fiction, are often "safe"—inventive perhaps in gadgetry, but conventional in theme, character, plot, and form. McCaffrey's *Restoree* is an unconventional novel by any standards. Understandably, it does not demonstrate the command of form McCaffrey shows in later work—the Pern novels or *The Crystal Singer*. But as a first published novel, it was not just promising, but unusual and iconoclastic, worth studying as representative of McCaffrey's evolution as a writer, but interesting in its own right for plot and imagery.

Decision at Doona, though it shares the premise of first-contact with *Restoree* and though it also represents narrative experimentation, impresses the reader as a more polished work. Indeed, *Restoree* was based on a story McCaffrey had written in the 1950s, though her novel version changes the entire approach of the story. But *Decision at Doona* has more memorable characters and is written more tightly. It also uses rather clever, unreliable narration.

The basic story is that Ken and Pat Reeve, with their children Ista and Todd, have been chosen to colonize Doona. They are ecstatic because wilderness area on overpopulated Earth has been reduced to twelve square miles. However, they encounter aliens called Hrrubans. This event is a disaster because Terran officials have promulgated a noninterference policy toward sentient aliens following the mass suicide of a sentient race contacted by Earthlings. Disappointed, the Reeves prepare to return to overcrowded Earth. Todd, however, forms a close bond with an alien child, and the aliens and colonists manage to arrange things so Hrrubans and humans can coexist on Doona.

What no plot summary can communicate about *Decision at Doona*, however, is the extent to which it is an endorsement of the natural world and a plea for allowing human imagination to range free. Todd Reeve, child-diplomat of the work, is a spirit who has adamantly refused to be shackled by societal restraints. His Earth is far more repressed by mores and restrictions than our Earth. Overpopulation has necessitated the restraint of personal spirit to the point that Aisle Proctors (like fifties housemothers) enforce silence and shuffling restriction of movement.

Todd, a boisterous, imaginative, lively child, is unsuited for this type of environment. Yet he is a natural child, a very gifted child who learns a difficult alien language in a few days and instructs his elders on matters of alien protocol. He has little difficulty surviving in a hostile environment, surviving brushes with poisonous plants, angry *mda,* and near-drowning without injury—though his daring often gets the more timid children into trouble. His survival superiority is illustrated when he single-handedly brings home a little girl who has been poisoned by a local plant, then disobeys his parents to obtain a medicinal salve to save the little girl. His sister Ista, in contrast, cowers in the cabin, afraid even to mention to her mother that she hasn't been fed all day in the excitement (*DAD* 126).

Todd represents the strength of imagination in the human spirit and, touchingly, may have been modeled on McCaffrey's own son Todd—at least it is to Todd Johnson that the book is dedicated. Not surprisingly, McCaffrey links Todd Reeve with two of her standard symbols for the human imagination—birds and horses.

The bird motif is only glancingly applied to Todd. He and a group of Hrruban cubs trap *brrnas*—small game fowl—to celebrate the barn raising. Ken, Todd's father, says that so many have been captured that "his house seemed to have sprouted wings" (*DAD* 134). Landreau, the Spacedep officer who attempts to destroy the colonists' dream of natural, free living, refuses to eat the cooked *brrnas*—he doesn't want to accustom his taste to such delicacies when he will have to return to the imprisonment of his civilized spaceship and its dead, unimaginative food. Wings elsewhere in McCaffrey represent the imaginative gift; here the child Todd furnishes wings and the unimaginative adult Landreau refuses them.

However, the most elaborate imagery of the natural world in *Decision at Doona* has to do with horses—again invoking the horse-and-rider image that we encounter in so much of McCaffrey's work. Todd and the horses make their appearance on adjacent pages in *Decision at Doona* (*DAD* 65, 66). And while the father, Ken, learns through grit and determination to ride and care for the horses, the son, Todd, is a natural horseman, whose exuberance finds full play in riding and currying the animals (*DAD* 111–117). Later, it is the beauty of the horses that convinces the Hrruban leader, Hrruna, to promote the coexistence of his people with the Earth-lings (*DAD* 218). The truly visionary people in the book—Hrriss, Hrrula, Todd, and Hrruna himself—are lovers of horses. When Ken finally breaks his stifling conditioning and runs to the site of the Hrruban village to seek help, his flight is a mad gallop on the horse he has finally learned to handle—he is finally in command of his dream, a creature not just of law, order, and obedience, but of imagination.

The horses' smell is a leitmotif throughout the book, and odors in general are dominant images. Reeve, captive in the overcrowded Earthly city, is aware for the first time of the overpowering odor of humanity around him as he makes his way to tell Pat that they are headed for Doona and freedom. The colonists' worst oath is "Sweat it!" (*DAD* 10, 17), their worst epithet, "smelly" (*DAD* 177). The Hrrubans themselves are odorous to human nostrils (*DAD* 34) and sensitive to other types of odors (*DAD* 32). Gaynor, who is slower to adapt to the demanding freedom of Doona, is offended by Hrruban odors and actually becomes allergic to the scent (*DAD* 57). The plant life of Doona has a pleasant, cinnamon odor, but the snakes, restive and id-like, have an overpoweringly unpleasant scent that makes the horses hysterical (*DAD* 186). The horses themselves, symbols of imagination set free, smell "not at all unpleasant" (*DAD* 64) and perhaps even sharpen Ken's appreciation of his own wife's scent (*DAD* 65).

Much more could be said about the imagery of the book. Reeve's name suggests Chaucer's carpenter, and he is a builder of a bridge between two villages—and two races. The tails of the Hrrubans are significant as evidence of their own animal natures, just as Ken's animal spirits are evidenced through his sense of smell.

But another important artistic device in the book is its use of ironic narration. Chapters I, VI, VII, and XXIII depict scenes on the Hrruban home-planet. However, because McCaffrey has created parallel situations on the Hrruban home-planet and Earth, the reader can easily *mistake* the setting in chapters I and VI, not understanding that the *Hrruban,* not Terran, leaders are debating the fate of Doona. Of course, the list of characters given before the table of contents would prevent this misunderstanding, but many readers do not carefully read such prefatory material and are apt to regard it with even more surprise when they consult it after finally figuring out what is going on.

The surprise in the book, of course, is that the Hrrubans are not innocent, nomadic forest-dwellers upon whom the colonists have happened accidentally. If they were such, Terran law requires that the colonists abandon their new, happy dwelling and return to dreary Earth or perhaps even be conscripted to an inhospitable mining planet. Since the Hrrubans have a very similar law, the reader naturally assumes that chapters I and VI show *Terran* leaders debating the fate of the colony. The first clues, other than the "characters" list itself, that the Hrrubans are space-travelers and not indigenous to Doona occurs when Ken realizes that Hrruban is a pitched language and observes that languages with pitch usually come from old civilizations. However, McCaffrey really tips her hand in chapter VIII when she speaks of "units . . . withdrawn" (*DAD* 53), a reference to the matter transmitter, which Terrans do *not* have. The appearance of Hrral (*DAD* 59) in the colony takes on significance when he coughs to avoid laughing at the assertion that he's unfamiliar with space travel. Hrral is the Senior Scout Chief who reports to First Speaker (Hrruna) in chapter VIII. We could follow a series of such hints, growing stronger and stronger, to the instantaneous disappearances of the Hrruban colonists, with Ken's ironic "You'll catch on, Ben, you'll catch on" (*DAD* 162) to the mystified Ben Adjei and, finally, his outright assertion, "The Hrrubans are not native to this planet" (*DAD* 170). The next Hrruban scene, in chapter XXIII, then clarifies the location of the first three such scenes by using personal names.

"Mystery" plots in science fiction are not uncommon, but McCaffrey, by concealing the setting and identity of characters in chapters I, VI, and for some readers (I admit to being so naive) VIII, uses an especially clever narrative twist.

Subtle use of unreliable narration also pertains to Todd Reeve. The boy is introduced first as a thorn in his parents' sides, writhing in the arms of a woman who thrusts him belligerently at his father. As we gradually begin to see him more and more as a natural child with splendid gifts, superior in his verve and imagination to other Terran children, McCaffrey is also changing our point of view and celebrating, through character development, the qualities that she exalts in later characters, such as the enterprising Helva, the headstrong Lessa, the dauntless Moreta, the plucky Jaxom, and the daring Killashandra. This vitality is a characteristic that she also honors through various forms of the horse-and-rider metaphor, which we will explore in chapters to come.

Restoree and *Decision at Doona* are books about the ingenuity and courage of a woman and a child. Their imagery and their experimentation with form lend them special value in the McCaffrey canon. They represent early examples of her narrative gift, her imagery, and her value system.

NOTES

[1] Anne McCaffrey, "Hitch Your Dragon to a Star: Romance and Glamour in Science Fiction," in *Science Fiction, Today and Tomorrow*, ed. Reginald Bretnor (New York: Harper & Row, 1974), p. 278.

[2] Quoted in Ed Naha, "Living with Dragons: Anne McCaffrey," *Future*, No. 6 (November 1978), p. 23.

[3] McCaffrey in Bretnor, p. 282.

[4] Mary T. Brizzi, "Narcissism and Romance in McCaffrey's *Restoree*," in *Patterns of the Fantastic*, ed. Donald M. Hassler (Mercer Island, Washington: Starmont House, 1983), pp. 41–46.

[5] Naha, 74.

III
THE SHIP WHO SANG

McCaffrey calls *The Ship Who Sang* her favorite novel; certainly it is the one that has been the subject of the most serious critical comment. More words have been written about the dragon books, but mostly they constitute fannish adulation, plot summary for book selection, or explanations of the obvious. *The Ship Who Sang,* with its sequel "Honeymoon," is a gem among McCaffrey's works for its originality of concept and its structure.

McCaffrey's sources for the book were many; unconsciously, the book was formed from the horse-and-rider metaphor that pervades so much of her fiction. Similarly, McCaffrey's love of children, interest in healing and medical matters, and perpetual faith in the beauty of sexual love must have been impulses behind many incidents in the book. All McCaffrey's work is socially responsible at the same time that it promotes the idea of art as an expression of humanity's highest nature. Her distrust of religious hysteria and her profound distaste for drug addiction prompted some of the characters and situations.

McCaffrey specifically points out three factors in the genesis of the book: first, her father's death; second, a pulp story of the brain of a child cruelly used as a spare organ, not to make the child a free-functioning cyborg like Helva, but a computer for a space shuttle; third, McCaffrey's acquaintance with the mother of a child with cerebral palsy.

In this chapter, I would like to deal with three basic critical questions. The first, represented by Andrew Gordon[1] who calls Helva a "mechanical Flying Nun," is that somehow the book isn't "science fiction" enough. Somehow, he feels, McCaffrey fails to come to terms with the horrific aspects of cyborgization. He compares *The Ship Who Sang* unfavorably with Samuel Delany's *Nova* and Frederik Pohl's *Man Plus.* Isaac Asimov[2] speaks well of *The Ship Who Sang,* but says a more sophisticated and subtle plot device would occur with purely mechanical intelligence.

The second critical question deals with sentimentality in the book. Some commentators purport to be revolted by Niall's passionate embrace of Helva's metal column as disgusting, unrealistic, or maudlin.

A third critical issue concerns the unity of the book. A motif that recurs in reviews and critiques is an offhand comment that *The Ship Who Sang* is a "collection of stories."[3] I have never seen a critical article defending the essential unity of the book, as I plan to do below.

The question of whether McCaffrey writes true science fiction and the question of whether her work is too sentimental are inextricably woven together and represent a larger issue treated in the conclusion of this study. The charges of "unscientificness," or failure to deal with the strictures of technical reality, on the other hand, have to be treated on a book-to-book basis. A few general comments, however, are appropriate here. Most attacks on McCaffrey's science are based on a failure to understand that science fiction, for McCaffrey, is primarily fiction and not an essay out of *Science Today* or *Omni*. McCaffrey's dictum is "Know more about your world than you actually tell," probably conceived from theatrical training: Method acting in print. McCaffrey creates a world so completely that she knows just what will happen in any situation. She doesn't explain everything in that world, but she herself *could* explain it. If a detail of world-sculpting, a scientific explanation, impedes the action rather than providing delight and wonder, then McCaffrey ruthlessly cuts it out. The woman is technologically and scientifically literate, but she regards herself *first* as a storyteller.

The other comment that needs to be made about McCaffrey's science is that she is fundamentally an optimist. She feels that people are human, that humans are more interesting than machines, and that a properly functioning human will ultimately be happy. Moreover, she believes in the adaptability of human beings. In Helva's case, this means that if you take a crippled little baby girl, alter her metabolism, surgically reroute her nervous system, and place her in a huge powerful ship used as an extension of her own body, that little girl will sing with joy to discover that she can tool around the Carina-Cygnus arm of the galaxy at several times the speed of light. Moreover, that little girl will quite naturally look for a lover when she reaches maturity—and somehow she will get one. These assumptions are optimistic; I think most writers who see McCaffrey as sentimental simply cannot conceive that human nature is so adaptable.

Science, in McCaffrey's world, exists to make people happy. Despite accidents, scientists, scholars, and technicians are fundamentally smart, good people who can and will rescue people from sickness, disaster, and despair and who have the power and inclination to improve human happiness. Pessimists might label such a radical statement Pollyannaism—but Helva is the manifestation of that optimism.

There are two technical premises behind *The Ship Who Sang*: one, the idea of a cyborg; two, the f. t. l. drive and the Corviki c. v. adaptation.

The nature of Helva's birth defect is left unexplored. We know that her adult body, even after surgical and chemical alteration, has a beautiful face—at least so Parollan believes. McCaffrey omits identifying the actual cause of the defect because someone would be sure to discover a way to prevent that particular defect before the publication of the first story. The first story hints at pure ugliness—McCaffrey's ugly duckling theme.

Cyborgs have been used in science fiction before, as discussed in Dunn and Erlich's collection *The Mechanical God*. McCaffrey's use of the concept is, however, original and striking. Helva is bright, talented, well-adjusted, and assertive. But, in contrast to most cyborgs, she is not an outsider (in Colin Wilson's sense) nor is she a superwoman. If she had been born in the twentieth century without a birth defect, we can imagine her cruising the malls for designer jeans or trying the latest fad diet, an aspiring career woman and a fine musician, a superior specimen, yes, but not a freak, not an alien, not Wonder Woman, not an Outsider.[4] She is one of us, except—she happens to be an interstellar starship.

This is what is novel about McCaffrey's treatment of the cyborg theme. She brings it home to us; we could have been cyborgs. The characters in Delany's superb *Nova*, by contrast, are exotic and extraordinary, not the girl and boy next door. The ordinariness of Helva's psychology is exactly what makes the cyborg treatment original and refreshing.

McCaffrey is quite aware that the sexual angle is an outstanding example of this novelty. Helva's guardians, those who adapted her to her titanium shell, neglected to provide either suppression of sexuality or opportunity for its expression. As with the virginal Daphnis and Chloe in the Greek romance, the enjoyment, the infatuation, the devotion is there, but consummation is impossible. The bizarre and moving scene in which Niall Parollan wraps himself around the metal column that contains Helva's deformed, stunted, and paralyzed body is breathtaking, though some critics profess to be repulsed by it. Reader revulsion often reveals that the writer has touched upon a universal emotion, has made an artistic statement of originality and power. Niall's fixation, with all its naked potential for destructiveness or creative joining, embarrasses us because it is a very real portrait of sexual obsession. As with Humbert Humbert's obsession with Lolita, its grotesqueness evokes the power of sexual love to shatter social icons and efface the lover's dignity.

This strange scene further emphasizes Helva's ordinary humanity. Parollan is not in love with a voice or with an immensely powerful vehicle. Despite clever humor in Gary Wolfe's assertion that "Helva has in some sense become Parollan's wife, but in a more real sense, she has become his house,"[5] Parollan is interested in the flesh and blood Helva. He personalizes her from the beginning and visualizes her physical body, as when he calls her "half-grown, wire-haired" (*SWS* 228). At the end of "Dramatic Mission," he threatens her with assignments that are "for the woman inside that armor plate." His references to her metal-protected virginity are quite literally sexual. In the climactic scene, Parollan is hugging that column; he is twitching to release the lock that places steel and titanium between him and the very flesh of his beloved. He has gone to great lengths to find out what her actual physical face looks like. The fact that she is paralyzed, deformed, and stunted to the size of a six-year-old child deters him not at all. He resembles a man who has fallen in love with a woman he has heard only over the telephone, fallen in love with her because of her courage, her talent, her wit, all the while knowing that she's a cripple. The only thing that deters him from uttering the release syllables is the fact that he knows he'll never commune with her again if he does— for her, unpleasant; for him, a criminal act.

This unresolved sexual situation caused fans to besiege McCaffrey for a sequel, as she explains in her introduction to "Honeymoon" in *Get Off the Unicorn.* Consummation occurs, of a type that would leave any human sexual experience a distinct disappointment: Helva and Niall actually merge with each other in Corviki envelopes. The physicality of the act is emphasized by the fact that when they separate into human bodies again, they discover that parts of their nervous systems somehow have become interchanged, and Helva can smell and taste things as Niall consumes them. Even in this story, however, Helva does not become a transcendent entity, a superhuman. She is only the same girl next door, made even more human by the ability to savor coffee.

The other major use of scientific lore in *The Ship Who Sang*—besides the Corviki envelopes and the various drugs such as mind trap, Menkalite, and Tucanite—involves attention to space travel itself. Science-fiction readers expect some sort of f. t. l. (faster-than-light) drive in any extrater-restrial adventure story because modern science depicts our solar system as inhospitable to intelligent life. Since the theoretical limit to the speed of light forbids travel to nearby stars in less than four to one-hundred years, McCaffrey uses the f. t. l. convention. However, her new twist is that Helva's top speed is about ten to twenty times the speed of light. This limitation renders a trip to the Horsehead nebula, for instance, beyond her technology unless she is willing to endure about a hundred years of travel time. She does not explore the time paradoxes that other writers, like Orson Scott Card for example, utilize. Nor does she estimate the accelera-tion forces required in reaching the speed of light, though there is vague reference to shock webs to cushion her passengers. She also assumes the use of an instantaneous communications device to connect Helva with her base—the device that ultimately makes possible her romance with Niall Parollan. In the end, of course, she obtains a new experimental drive that permits travel at perhaps fifteen times her previous top velocity (*SWS* 215) or 150 to 300 times the speed of light, making a light year a matter of a day's travel. I am, by the way, extrapolating these figures from the various chapters of the book in a way that McCaffrey did not intend. But she apparently researched astronomy enough to at least create an illusion that results of the calculations—if somebody cared to do them—would not be entirely ludicrous.

Surprisingly, of the fifty-eight proper names associated with astronomi-cal bodies in the book plus the story "Honeymoon," forty-one actually correspond with items in *Burnham's Celestial Handbook* (which, as a com-plete amateur, I found most useful in explaining stellar matters).[6] Ten appear to be named associatively, and seven appear to be syllable con-structs. McCaffrey need not have been so meticulous; few, other than hobbyists and professionals in astronomy, would know that some may be pure coinage, but Tucana (*SWS* 189) is a real constellation. Most of the coinages appear in the first two episodes; in "The Ship Who Killed," the sixteen named bodies all correspond to items in *Burnham's Handbook*, and there is some evidence that McCaffrey researched their proximity to each other to imply that Kira and Helva speed from one to another with their baby-cargo. The stars of the visited planets all appear to be part of a large system in Ursa Major, while Alioth, the planet where Kira is kidnapped by a mad rogue brain ship, is apparently named after the star Alioth, Epsilon Ursae Majoris. McCaffrey suggests enough names that the journeys of Helva and her brawns have verisimilitude. She uses the star names in a scientific sense as a writer of historical novels might use details of couture, cuisine, or conversation to lend authenticity.

This is the use of science to produce an artistic effect—one of the methods of creating the sense of wonder. However, once McCaffrey had discovered the wealth of lore behind star names, she used it symbolically. Naturally, some references will be quite obvious. Regulus suggests a ruler, and so Regulus is the base planet of Central Worlds. The fact that Nekkar, the planet awaiting Helva's cargo of human embryos, is in the constellation Bootes suggests a pun on the "booties" that these babies will soon wear. Scorpius is mentioned in the same breath with the machinations of the scorpion-like Ansra Colmer. The use of the Horsehead nebula as a dream-goal for Helva and her beloved evokes McCaffrey's ever-present horse-and-rider metaphor, apparent also in the dragon books, in *To Ride Pegasus* and even in Helva's own situation.

A little knowledge of astronomy, however, yields additional allusive power. Helva's very first mission is to Spica—a star in Virgo, the virgin. The imagery is picked up and echoed in reference not just to the virgin voyage, but to Niall's bantering references to Helva's metallically protected virginity. Betelgeuse is a central star in Orion, the eleventh brightest star in the sky, and a very large red giant: "The Armpit of the Giant." Appropriately, Sylvia, Helva's elder sister ship and mentor, refers to a great, nameless tragedy that took place near this impressive and distant star. "Dramatic Mission," the episode that begins with the vulture-like Ansra Colmer baiting the dying Solar Prane and ends with four lifeless bodies in Helva's cabins, takes place on a planet circling a star in Corvus, the constellation of the crow, a death-harbinger. The constellation Reticulum may have been named for cross hairs in an optical instrument, but the word also means *net,* and it is in the web of Reticulan croons that Helva traps the evil Xixon. When Kira and Helva (a *shell* person) are taking their egg-like cargo of human embryos to Nekkar, egg imagery is reflected in mention of the stars Beid and Keid, which are, according to tradition, the egg and the eggshell. The Ophiuchi circuit is forbidden to Kira because of her "dylanizing"—and dylanizing means influencing behavior with music. Ophiuchus is usually referred to as the "serpent holder," but some authorities made it the "serpent charmer"—someone who dylanizes snakes? Kira, by the way, is from Canopus, which means *the pilot*—and the implication is that after her trip with Helva she will continue training to become a scout.[7]

This is not to argue that star names have much to do with scientific fact. But McCaffrey did demonstrate superior artistic dedication in using real stars and researching their locations to fit the universe she has invented for Helva while using their names in imaginative symbolic ways. Of course, the fictional stars with historical and mythological names also have symbolic implications; most obviously, Medea (I do not find a star named Medea in any catalogue available to me), the home of Theoda, is the plague-planet, which instead of being a kindly mother Earth, murdered its own children. Van Gogh is the site of a more current tragedy, reflecting the torment in the painter's life; also Van Gogh painted a very striking painting of Ursa Major. Coined names for stars and planets are quite realistic because in Helva's future world many new planets and even stars will be discovered.

McCaffrey could have made up all her star names without researching whether a brain ship traveling at ten times the speed of light could travel from star A to star B without an undue hiatus in the plot, or she might simply have used black holes or hyperspace drives or even psychokinesis to transport her characters from one scene to another—honorable solutions to the fictional problem. But McCaffrey did it the hard way, and the book is more original for it. Moreover, the earthy, very physical tone of Helva's world, where we never totally forget how things ought to feel or taste—even though we have to find out from Helva's brawns—is reinforced by this sense of place and distance. To be sure, the details of the Corviki cycle-variant drive are mostly verbal sleight-of-hand. But again, they are done by using the vocabulary of particle physics in a poetic way, to suggest and to stimulate the imagination, rather than coldly to explain. These passages have the same kind of appeal as the Corviki thought patterns that Helva and her associates adopt during transfer.

Also, McCaffrey does take one major liberty with reality. The Horsehead nebula, which has remained a dream of Helva's since her first days with Jennan, is not a galaxy, as implied in "The Partnered Ship" (*SWS* 213). It is, although relatively much more distant from Regulus than Helva's other destinations, within our galaxy. I feel McCaffrey wrote herself into a corner here; she used the Horsehead nebula originally because of its romantic photographic appearance and her fascination with the horse-and-rider motif. Later, the image was too good to abandon, even though it didn't fit the model of intergalactic travel she needed.

Charges of sentimentality are a second point of controversy with this novel, as they are with all McCaffrey's work. They will never be fully resolved, simply because McCaffrey is unwilling to compromise her point of view on sex and romance, which tends to be unpopular with cynics of both sexes. She pities those who live "in quiet desperation, on the off-chance that there might be a moment, of beauty, of love, tomorrow" (*SWS* 234). She feels these moments of beauty are accessible to human beings through rather conventional channels. She is not averse to peculiar adaptations of these channels to particular circumstances (dragonriders have unusual sex lives), and therefore if Helva can only have a partner who has a rather peculiar fixation, a partner with whom there can be no true consummation, that is the way that Helva should go. It would be ludicrous, in McCaffrey's terms, to pretend that Helva's greatest joy in life will *not* come from human relations.

Once we admit the premises that one of life's greatest joys is a conventional love relationship, that the pursuit of this goal is a proper topic for fiction, and that children are magical receptacles for our values and future, *The Ship Who Sang* isn't sentimental. Additionally, Helva has many other interests besides her love life, although two of the stories do use this as a prime plot mover. Moreover, McCaffrey uses irony to undercut sentimentality.

For example, Niall Parollan is the least "romance novel" hero in McCaffrey's works. An egotistical, sarcastic, even obnoxious runt, his constant jibes at Helva's titanium-protected virginity are rather too coarse for the most risque of romance novels. He refers to her at one point in the book as "tin-assed" (*SWS* 228); his comments and behavior in "Honeymoon" are quite crude. Her first olfactory sensation on emerging from the Corvikian envelope in "Honeymoon" is the stench of his unwashed body. His first name, Niall, means *champion*, a pleasantly romantic touch. However, *Parollan* reminds me a great deal of Parolles in Shakespeare's *All's Well That Ends Well*. The parallels may well be conscious. Parolles' first appearance occasions a contest of wits with Helena on the topic of virginity, a more serious issue later in the play. Niall Parollan, similarly, constantly jokes about Helva's virginity, which likewise becomes an issue in his relationship with her. The similarities are underlined in similarities between Shakespeare's Helena and McCaffrey's Helva. Helena wins the regard of the court as a healer. Helva, too, participates in several healing episodes, from the healing of Kira's morbidity to helping Theoda find a cure for the Van Gogh plague to permitting the transfer of Solar Prane's psyche from a diseased body to a healthy Corviki envelope. Helena is offered her choice of husband as reward for her services. Helva is offered her choice of brawn. Both find their choices of partner reluctant. Parolles, however, is a liar and a coward, neither of which Niall Parollan is. Niall Parollan, in fact, is more a cross between Bertram and Parolles—with, we admit, a little romance hero thrown in. His melodramatic disappearance, to save Helva from the bad bargain into which he believes he has weaseled her, does smack a bit of the impetuous hero of the typical romance, who does bad things because he loves the heroine so much. But McCaffrey must be touching a responsive chord in readers: Niall is a sympathetic character.

McCaffrey's irony is often subtle to a fault. So with Parollan's dialogue with her after the Xixon episode. She asks:
"Catch up on your beauty sleep?"
"Both."
"Both?"
"Both beauty and sleep."
[The beauty, of course, is not some rival, but Helva herself, with whom Parollan has just "caught up."]
"She didn't mind your snoring?"
"*They* were too exhausted to hear much and too grateful to comment." *They* in fact were not necessarily Niall's paramours, but other members of Cencom who were happy that Niall had been able to trace Helva and aid in her rescue. Even in "Honeymoon," it isn't clear that Parollan's reputation for womanizing is entirely deserved. Niall then continues his teasing:
"I pick *my* partners carefully, not just for the symmetry of their features and density of their skulls."
Helva, his ultimate choice, is not conventionally attractive. The whole

conversation could imply Niall's licentiousness, but it also implies his fixation on Helva.

Sentimentality about children is also a danger in this novel, but McCaffrey's treatment of the episode in which Onro's son is being repatterned to cure his paralysis shows a rather unsentimental use of irony. Theoda, having done her best, is fussing over the child, Onro is pleading, and Helva drawls, "Come on, Momma's sweet little freckle-faced boy" (*SWS* 47), so sarcastically that the child moves out of anger.

A final example of antisentimental irony requires a bit of knowledge of music. Helva sings to Kira, "Music for awhile/Shall all your cares beguile/Wondering how your pains were eased" (*SWS* 66), a pleasant enough lyric, unless you happen to know the context: it is from the Dryden-Lee libretto to Purcell's *Oedipus*. Demons tormenting the damned are being invoked. The lyric continues, "Till Alecto free the dead/From their eternal bands;/Till the snakes drop from her head,/And whip from out her hands."[8] The lyric neatly foreshadows the inferno-like scenes on Alioth and provides a motivation for Kira's explosion of despair.

The charge of sentimentality is one that needs a book-by-book defense; McCaffrey's ironic touches are often so subtle that they seem overbalanced by the seeming conventionality of her love scenes.

A final critical issue is whether *The Ship Who Sang* is indeed a novel or a collection of short stories. McCaffrey says that she conceived the basic premise in 1958. Writing and publication of the six sections, or episodes, took place over a period of eleven years; "The Ship Who Sang" appeared in *Fantasy and Science Fiction* in 1961; the book, with a final piece and some editing of the magazine sections, did not appear until 1969. In between, the other episodes appeared in *If, Galaxy,* and *Analog.* Examination of the serial versions shows minor, but careful editing. *Scout* has been changed to *brawn* in the book form for consistency. An addition has been made at the end of the fourth section, "Dramatic Mission," showing an encounter between Niall and Helva. A few sections have been deleted. Helva's interior monologues have been strengthened by switching to first person. The changes are not fundamental, and yet the book form demonstrates essential unity that argues that it be called a novel rather than a collection of stories.[9]

The unity of *The Ship Who Sang* expresses itself through consistency and development of character throughout. Helva begins the novel, at age sixteen, as a polite, but very self-confident, professional lady. Ten years later, she is even more self-confident, but a bit brassier, canny in her negotiations with Central Worlds. Her optimism has not been permanently quelled by the death of her first love nor by the fact that in ten years she has found no one to replace him in her heart. Despite mature moments of questioning, she acts like a bright, young career woman with ten years of success behind her.

Niall represents more of a problem. It isn't clear that he enters the narrative until the end of "Dramatic Mission." The voice that guides her from Cencom in earlier episodes does show some of the asperity of the later Parollan, as in "The Ship Who Killed" when Cencom demands: "May-day? . . . You bet—with a cratty fool dylanizing on Alioth?" (*SWS* 85). Even the Cencom that answers Onro's call in "The Ship Who Mourned" seems shocked and disappointed to hear someone besides Helva (*SWS* 33).

Only one other character, aside from Chief Railly, appears at the beginning and end of the book, and this is Silvia, who is both a mentor and an object-lesson to Helva. In both her scenes with Helva, she offers homely advice, compassion, and a bit of cynicism.

Other characters are mentioned again after their appearance; so with Kira, Helva's favorite brawn after Jennan and Parollan; so with the members of the dramatic embassy to Beta Corviki. The SL 732 is described in the first episode and appears (as the mad rogue ship on Alioth) in the third episode. McCaffrey uses these allusions to tie the narrative together. Interestingly, many of these narrative links exist in the magazine versions of the episodes, indicating that McCaffrey may have had in mind a whole book, at least subconsciously, from the beginning.

The plot, too, suggests a unified action. Each section functions as a short story, with its own discrete problem, conflict, climax, and resolution. But the solution to each problem ties in with the rest of the book and contributes to the solution to Helva's ultimate problem, the finding of a permanent partner. For example, the Corviki episode establishes Helva's ability to maintain individual awareness without falling to pieces when sense-deprived by Xixon, which in turn suggests her as the right ship to return to Corviki as a final assignment, which allows her to demand Parollan as her brawn. Moreover, it is the Corviki who enable Central Worlds to develop their modified f. t. l. drive.

The basic action of the book, however, is love, loss of love, and growth to a new, more mature love. "The Ship Who Sang" is, of course, about the loss of love. "The Ship Who Mourned" shows Helva released from debilitating grief over Jennan. "The Ship Who Killed" enables her to raise her self-esteem by seeing how another, the 732, is destroyed by grief and by helping another, Kira, overcome grief. "Dramatic Mission" expands Helva's awareness of the types of love relationships possible—the bitter love of Ansra Colmer, the self-sacrificial love of Kurla Ster, etc. "The Ship Who Dissembled" gives Helva a model of what *not* to look for in a partner and also suggests that she is herself loved, even though she ignores the hint at the time. "The Partnered Ship," of course, shows her finally finding a new love. All of the episodes show how an artistic temperament and love of adventure contribute to the sort of person who ultimately becomes a successful lover. Her partnership with Parollan is based on their mutual confidence in each other, their humor, and their love of challenge.

Thematically and symbolically, too, the book shows unity. Themes of physical and spiritual healing, themes of children and reproduction, allusions to fictional lovers, and McCaffrey's unique view of the role of art all unify the book.

The theme of healing pervades the book. Helva herself begins life as a cripple; science and human ingenuity make her whole. Her mission with Theoda is a healing mission, and here McCaffrey borrows from the controversial Doman-Delacato technique of repatterning, which has been used in our day with autistic and learning-disabled children, and models Theoda on Elizabeth Kenny, who discovered an early successful polio therapy. Kira, in "The Ship Who Killed," is emotionally sick, but she also has a physical ailment—she is sterile—and Helva suggests a possible alternative to her sterility. The ironic Macbeth quotation about Kira's child "untimely ripped" from its mother's womb contrasts nicely with the gentle *Romeo and Juliet* quotations later in the book. Kurla Ster is a healer figure in "Dramatic Mission," though the cure of Solar Prane ultimately proves radical. The illness in "The Ship Who Dissembled" is drug addiction; the Xixon learns too late that the cure is death. Nobody is really sick in "The Partnered Ship," but the continued reference to Helva as "dead" (*SWS* 167) or in a "coffin" (*SWS* 229) finally reaches a climax as Parollan is able to accept the fact that his love, though living, is forever physically inaccessible.

The children motif runs through the early episodes only, but it is an important motif generally in McCaffrey. McCaffrey's love of children is utterly unsentimental. There is nothing cute about the embryonic "babies in ribbons" Helva carries to Nekkar, nor is Onro's crippled son at all sweet—he's just a "young hellion" with a paralytic disease. Of course, Helva is first seen as a baby, then a child. Her polite naivete, when confronted with the first nonshelled people, is delightful and amusing.

The motif of lovers in the novel is underscored in both obvious and subtle ways. Of course, the extended use of quotations from *Romeo and Juliet* in "Dramatic Mission," with ironic comparisons to the dramatic company playing these roles, contributes to the effect. Helva's cabin at the end of this episode, like the stage at the end of Shakespeare's play, is strewn with lifeless bodies, both of lovers and others. But there are references to other Shakespearean lovers. Prane quotes Miranda as well as Prospero—in *The Tempest* (*SWS* 148)—an interesting combination, considering Prane's December–May relationship with Kurla! Davo's taunt, "hath desire outstripped performance then?" (*SWS* 116) echoes lines in The Porter's Scene in *Macbeth*, but I like to place it in Shakespeare's drama of faithless love, *Troilus and Cressida* (3.2.196) for characteristic McCaffrey irony. It is typical of McCaffrey to have Helva, who after all plays the Nurse, not Juliet, in "Dramatic Mission," to paraphrase the words of Rosalind in *As You Like It* (4.1.110) after Niall's disappearance in "The Partnered Ship": "Men have died, and worms have eaten them, but not for love" (*SWS* 231).

We have already discussed the echo in names between Helva and Helena in *All's Well That Ends Well*. The references to Helva's titanium shell also suggests another Shakespeare heroine, Titania. Like Titania, Helva has powers above those of an ordinary human; like Titania, she falls in love with a donkey—Teron—though her infatuation is well over by the time we see her at the beginning of "The Ship Who Dissembled." Silvia's name, too, is Shakespearean in allusion; she is the beloved of Valentine in *Two Gentlemen of Verona*.

Lovers of non-Shakespearean origin are also alluded to: Daphnis and Chloe are the major figures in a Greek romance by Longus and also in a ballet by Ravel; so in "The Ship Who Sang" McCaffrey ironically names a novaing sun Ravel and its two planets Daphnis and Chloe. For further irony, Chloe is far from a place of pastoral dalliance—it is occupied solely by female religious devotees, and its climate (until the nova) is frigid. Daphnis and Chloe in story and ballet are separated by pirates and other adventures but ultimately reunited to celebrate their marriage. Helva and Jennan are separated by death at the explosion of Ravel. Interestingly, the composer Ravel suffered late in life from aphasia, which made communication impossible for him—a parallel to the type of defect that Helva was born with or that afflicted the plague victims in "The Ship Who Mourned."

Helva does indulge herself by comparing her beauty to Helen of Troy (*SWS* 231); she also thinks, in that doubtful hour, of Cleopatra—not Shakespeare's mature, but insecure heroine—rather the young, impertinent Cleopatra of Shaw (*SWS* 237).

The very title of the novel suggests the importance of art and the artist in it, a theme which is developed throughout. Helva sings, and she is shown early in "The Ship Who Sang" copying "The Last Supper." Music is what draws Jennan and her together; she learns of his loyalty when he defends her title as singer. The ability to sing all different voice parts, indeed to produce musical sounds no ordinary organism could produce is a dream for the artist, the ultimate fantasy for a singer.

The romance of Helva and Jennan begins with a song, Purcell's "Come All Ye Sons of Art (Birthday Music for Queen Mary)," and ends with a ballet (alluded to in the planets Daphnis and Chloe). Her hours of mourning ("The Ship Who Mourned") are marked by a refusal to sing. She vanquishes a foe in "The Ship Who Killed" through music and administers therapy to her brawn likewise. "Dramatic Mission" permits her to get into acting as well as singing, and again her artistic talents bring riches to humanity, as the Corviki trade a new energy principle for old plays. In "The Ship Who Dissembled," she uses the tantalizing lure of beautiful music to tempt the Xixon to turn up her volume so that she can destroy his nervous system with "pure sonic hell" (*SWS* 191). She counters Teron early with quotations from Tennyson (*SWS* 177) and later with a softer version of the sonic fury she loosed on the Xixon. Then, she charms Niall with more music when comes to babysit her. The first episode and the last end with Helva singing taps, mournfully at first, then hopefully. Music and drama are insistently the central metaphor of the book.

Nor is art all high-tone. Helva, in a moment of panic in the lair of the Xixon, recites not just Shakespeare's *Romeo and Juliet* and Purcell's "I Attempt from Love's Fever to Fly" from Dryden's *The Indian Queen,* but also the beginning of a limerick, which she cannot finish because she has the first line wrong (*SWS* 185). The correct version is

> There was a young lady of Chichester
> Who made all the saints in their niches stir.
> One morning at matins
> Her breasts in white satins
> Made the Bishop of Chichester's britches stir.[10]

Although it would be tedious to indicate all of Helva's sources—she is especially fond of Purcell and Dryden—there is through all her commentary on art the assumption that art is one of the two forces that create happiness in human life (the other being human love) and the further assumption that art is by nature utilitarian—it exists to teach and create happiness. As a corollary, attention to the arts will yield long-term benefits. Helva's singing gets her the Corviki mission, and on a more homely level, her attention to redecorating her interior pays off in her wooing of Solar Prane's Shakespeare troupe.

The concept of dylanizing, explored mostly in "The Ship Who Mourned," makes clear the practical use of art. On the surface, dylanizing—the use of art to alter judgment and attitude—sounds dryly didactic. But McCaffrey's prime example is not so straightforward. Kira, in this episode, is haunted by a death wish—her lover has died; she is sterile and could never have his child, even by postmortem insemination. Central Worlds, although (probably because of the machinations of Niall Parollan) they don't explain why to Helva, forbid Kira to visit certain worlds, afraid that her death wish may be communicated to sensitive cultures and cause mass suicides. However, through an error, Alioth, with a death cult led by the rogue ship 732, is not interdicted. Kira becomes swept away with the overpowering religious intensity of the crowds. Helva rescues her only by playing upon the death wish of Alioth and of Kira—and forcing it to its ultimate absurdity by making her song of death ironic. This, Cencom admits, is real dylanizing.

McCaffrey dylanizes, too. Her work exists to make people happy and to make them think positively about the possibilities of life, art, adventure, the family, and the future.

The concept of payoff is relevant here. Part of the ongoing plot of the novel is the notion that Helva is required to pay back the money required for her expensive modification training. This concept exists in other McCaffrey novels as well; for example, Killashandra in *The Crystal Singer* is required to pay back the money for her crystal-singing apprenticeship. The pay-back concept seems to have an analogue in the Biblical tale of the talents. We all owe to our parents and society a debt for our early rearing and nurturance, which is paid back by our being useful members of society. For the artist, it means using the artistic gift fruitfully.

McCaffrey's interest in the role of the artist continues in the separate short story "Honeymoon," where the Asuran extrapolations bring Helva closer to self-knowledge, if only of her own face. The party that Niall and Helva throw is occasion for much art talk; later Helva whiles away the weary hours with Shakespeare, replicas of phallic art objects, and tapes of insect dances from Lyrae IV.

In her introduction to "Honeymoon," McCaffrey confesses that she identifies with Helva, and I think this identification is with Helva as artist. Perhaps in the continuation of "Honeymoon," she will explore the Corvikian culture, further extending the metaphor suggested by the use of the word *envelope* for the psychic receptacle the Corviki offer. After all, writers' artistic production spends a great deal of time in envelopes.

This chapter should end with some discussion of the use of the horse-and-rider metaphor that exists in so much of McCaffrey's work. With due respect for Gary Wolfe's admirable analysis of the spaceship metaphor, I think he has placed too much emphasis, at least in McCaffrey's case, on the coziness of the spaceship as vehicle. The horse-and-rider metaphor in this novel involves an organism composed of ship and rider, together a "Helluva" ship—Helva. This is an artistic metaphor: the rider is the artist, and the ship (or horse, or dragon) is the art form itself. The relationship between the two is intense, intimate, demanding, sometimes dangerous. The two, artist and art form, rider and horse, brain and ship, can go where mere mortals never can step. They are privileged people, who also do wonderful things to help and save ordinary humanity. They are special; in Helva's case the ugly duckling metaphor is related because Helva without her ship is a pitiful cripple. Had she been born healthy, she would never have become the great and powerful 834. Her bane was precious.

How does the brawn figure into this scheme? The metaphor seems much simpler in the pegasus and dragon books; in *The Ship Who Sang,* we are confronted with this other entity, a kind of superfluous rider who is not needed, but who helps, and I suspect that the brawn represents exactly that—an editor, an inspiration, an encouraging friend or lover.

It is a beautiful metaphor for a novel: it combines the themes McCaffrey desires, art and love. Niall and Jennan nurture and advise the central individual artist, Helva, in her daring and breathtaking adventures. The ship is the artistic medium, without which the artist is but a mundane, land-bound cripple. So nearly is the artist bound to her art, like brain and ship, that they become fused. In Peter Shaffer's *Equus,* Dysart tells Alan that Amerind natives, first seeing cavalry, thought man and horse were one being—a god. Later in the play, Alan elaborates that theme when he sees himself fused with Nugget, exultant in his identity as one person with the horse. So is Helva identified with her ship. So is the intense identification of artist and art. Together they transcend ordinary reality. The lover, the brawn, the friend is a witness, a mentor, and a helper in this flight into the unknown. The adventure that brain, ship, and brawn embark upon is infinite, spiritual, almost divine. Helva, at the end of "Honeymoon," may well sing hallelujahs.

Later in this study, we will see how this metaphor takes first psychic, then animate form, as "talent" and dragons become the representatives of art.

NOTES

[1] "Human, More or Less: Man-Machine Communion in Samuel R. Delany's *Nova* and Other Science Fiction Stories," in Thomas P. Dunn and Richard D. Erlich, eds., *The Mechanical God: Machine in Science Fiction* (Westport, CT: Greenwood, 1982), pp. 193–202.

[2] *Asimov on Science Fiction* (Garden City, NY: Doubleday, 1981), p. 146.

[3] See for example, Baird Searles, Martin Last, Beth Meacham, and Michael Franklin, *A Reader's Guide to Science Fiction* (New York: Avon, 1979), p. 117.

[4] The magazine version of "The Ship Who Dissembled" ("The Ship Who Dis-

appeared") indicates some original premises on her nervous system adaptation. Her olfactory and tactile senses are translated into atmospheric characteristics, etc.

[5] Gary K. Wolfe, *The Known and the Unknown: The Iconography of Science Fiction* (Kent, OH: Kent State University Press, 1979), pp. 83-84.

[6] Robert Burnham, Jr., *Burnham's Celestial Handbook: An Observer's Guide to the Universe beyond the Solar System,* 3 volumes (New York: Dover, 1978).

[7] Richard Hinckley Allen, *Star Names: Their Lore and Meaning* (New York: Dover, 1963). Although Allen's work, originally published in 1899, may represent etymologies now thought to be inaccurate, it does present the type of old etymology that McCaffrey draws upon, simply because it is popular and more likely to be known by her readers.

[8] John Dryden and Nathaniel Lee, *Oedipus,* in *Dryden: The Dramatic Works,* ed. Montague Summers (London: Nonesuch, 1932), IV, 351-427.

[9] "Honeymoon" is not logically a part of this novel because it does not form a part of the cycle of love, loss, mourning, regeneration, and discovery of new love. It might even be the first chapter of a new novel. Moreover, a set of new questions is introduced: Where do the Corviki get empty envelopes? How extensive is the ego-sharing between Helva and Niall? Will it forestall frustration and jealousy? What are the implications of the *cuy* particles? A sequel may explore heightened thought processes, theory of telepathy, and plot possibilities from McCaffrey's inventive use of particle physics.

[10] *The Limerick: 1700 Examples, with Notes, Variants, and Index. The Famous Paris Edition* (Secaucus, NJ: Castle Books, no date), p. 111.

IV

THE DRAGONRIDER BOOKS: PERN RENAISSANCE

This chapter deals with three major topics: the symbolism of Pern; the structure and symmetry of the two trilogies, *The Dragonriders of Pern* and the Harper Hall books; and finally the issue of feminism in the Pern novels and story. *The Dragonriders of Pern* comprises *Dragonflight*, *Dragonquest*, and *The White Dragon*; the Harper Hall trilogy is composed of *Dragonsong, Dragonsinger*, and *Dragondrums. A Time When* is an early version of part of *The White Dragon*. I will also allude to "The Smallest Dragonboy" and close with a discussion of the recently published *Moreta, Dragonlady of Pern*.

McCaffrey is writing about the social, political, and artistic renaissance of a semifeudal, semicommunistic society. To lend depth and power to the changes the renaissance makes in the life of the characters of the novels, she borrows extensively from symbolism of the poetry of William Butler Yeats, particularly the poems "The Second Coming," "Sailing to Byzantium," "Leda and the Swan," and "Byzantium"[1] —in other words, the most popular of Yeats's visionary poems.

The name *Pern* cannot have been chosen randomly. McCaffrey is Irish; her mind as she developed Pern and its dragons was on things Irish; and she chose a word from the mythos of an Irish poet for the name of the planet of dragons. In "Sailing to Byzantium," Yeats invokes "sages standing in God's holy fire," these being prophets of art whom he seeks as teachers, to "Come from the holy fire, perne in a gyre." A *perne* (or *pirn*, as spelled in the N. E. D.) is a kind of bobbin used in weaving; a *gyre* is a spiral, or in Yeats's metaphysics, a cone-shaped path representing the cyclic passage of history. Specifically, in Yeats's work, two gyres were supposed to interpenetrate, each representing antithetical ideas.[2] McCaffrey's Pern is indeed in a gyre—the orbit it describes around its sun, Rukbat. The other gyre is the orbit of the Red Star, which periodically intercepts Pern's orbit, causing tectonic upheavals, unusual weather patterns, and, most important, the fall of deadly Thread.

These upheavals, in Yeats's cosmology, occur at 2000-year intervals—"Twenty centuries of stony sleep," as he puts it in "The Second Coming." On McCaffrey's Pern, upheavals occur at intervals of only two-hundred years, although there has been an atypical interval, 400 years, at the beginning of *Dragonflight*. Other marvels, both good and bad, accompany the period of disruption, or Pass, as the period of Thread-fall is called. A dying queen dragon lays an egg from which issues a particularly large queen, Ramoth. The ability of dragons to time-travel is discovered, and the mystery of the lost Weyrs is solved along with the Riddle Song. Dragonmen fight each other, as F'lar does T'ron and later T'kul. A queen egg is stolen; there is talk of dragon fighting dragon and of dragons flaming innocent Holders. Most important, people of extraordinary courage, ingenuity, and leadership ability emerge to save Pern from Thread and to turn the threat of the Red Star into an opportunity for cultural advancement: Lessa, F'lar, Robinton, Menolly, and others. Cultural stagnation has set in on Pern, but the Present Pass encourages gold dragons to fly against Thread, Impressions to be made of a green dragon by a woman rider, and a Holder to Impress a mutant dwarf white dragon. Innovation in the arts, mostly the subject of the Harper Hall trilogy, is also stimulated: Menolly, a woman, is allowed advancement in a male-dominated field; new subjects are allowed for epic music; compositions of a nontraditional form are permitted, as those of Menolly and Domick. By the end of the Dragonriders trilogy, the rediscovery of old knowledge and the advance of new permit the use of microscope, telescope, paper, telegraph, etc. In fact, the swiftness of these revolutionary cultural advances would seem implausible except that Pern has no religious hierarchy to impede scientific progress. Finally, a new species is discovered—fire lizards.

Lessa, at the beginning of the trilogy, resembles the persona of "The Second Coming." The watchweyr, like Yeats's falcon "turning and turning in the widening gyre," circles restlessly (*DF* 1). Lessa is roused by a feeling of foreboding from the East (which is where the Red Star rises). Her "ceremony of innocence" has surely been drowned by the usurpation of Fax. His untraditional attempt to hold more than one Hold has resulted in "mere anarchy"; "things fall apart; the centre cannot hold," not only because of Fax's cruelty, but because Lessa has been using psychic powers to ruin Ruatha Hold and more broadly, because of the approach of the Red Star. Of course, the literal threat is Lessa's own older self, time traveling, which rouses her at that dawn, but the Red Star, which is shortly to be so near that it is visible in daylight, could correspond to the Yeatsean shape with "gaze blank and pitiless as the sun." The horror of the Red Star is fully revealed when F'nor attempts to fly *between* to it so as to attack Thread at the source, and the Red Star, in the East like Bethlehem in Yeats's poem, corresponds to the "rough beast."

The circular image implied in Yeats's word *gyre* seems to be picked up throughout both trilogies. Not only does the watchweyr circle at the beginning of *Dragonflight*, but dragons almost always circle to land, and lizards fly in circles and spirals. The eyes of both dragons and fire lizards whirl whenever something important is going to happen. Fax and Gemma both wear rings—another circular image—and when Gemma is giving birth, her rings bite into Lessa's hands as she grips her (*DF* 50). Menolly, one of the most important people on the planet (if McCaffrey were ever forced to depict Robinton's death, she'd have to make Menolly the new Masterharper), comes from Half-*Circle* Sea Hold. The word for a year on Pern is *Turn*—capitalized, as if bearing some sort of sacred significance. Jaxom's assertion of his rights as Holder in *The White Dragon* are likened to a stone's falling in water to spread ripples—a circular pattern (*WD* 148, 296).

Yeats frequently refers to a birth as the beginning of a new cycle of history. A "rough beast" is born at the end of "The Second Coming"; Leda is impregnated by Zeus in "Leda and the Swan." Birth is one of the most powerful images in the dragon books. The Hatching of Ramoth, for example, is probably the most widely read piece of writing McCaffrey has ever done, and it won her her first Nebula and Hugo. The day Lessa is taken on Search, Jaxom is born. His irregular birth is echoed later in the Hatching of his dragon Ruth. The Hatching of other dragons and of fire lizards are points of particular interest in the series: Mirrim's Path, K'van's Heth, Menolly's nine fire lizards, Robinton's, Sebell's, Piemur's, and even Kylara's and Meron's fire lizards—the births of all these are powerfully emotional images. It is our inclination anyway to be awed at the emergence of new life, but McCaffrey makes these births more significant through their impact on the history of Pern. The best case in point is the Hatching of Ramoth.

McCaffrey uses a number of techniques to create a greater sense of wonder at the Hatching of Ramoth. It is a surprise, as births often are—Lessa is unprepared. We aren't sure Lessa is going to get, or even wants, the dragon. The fact that Ramoth herself instinctively knows her own name and tells it to Lessa gives the dragon a supernatural aura. The name itself cannot fail to remind us of Ra, the Egyptian sun-god. Ramoth accidentally kills two women in the process of finding Lessa, another surprise. Nor are we prepared for the flood of emotion Lessa feels at beholding Ramoth's "rainbow regard."

But McCaffrey also draws upon Yeatsean imagery to intensify the sense of wonder. Lessa herself resembles Leda of "Leda and the Swan"— the names are only two letters different. Like Leda, she is suddenly taken by something with "great wings"—a dragon, rather than the Yeatsean swan. The ultimate consequence of this seizure will be a social unheaval like the Yeatsean "broken wall, the burning roof and tower,/And Agamemnon dead." Though Lessa doesn't actually lay an egg, her impact on Pern's history is dependent on the Egg of Ramoth and on subsequent eggs laid by Ramoth. The explicit sexual experience in the Yeats' poem is not quite a rape—Leda's thighs do "loosen"—but is certainly unexpected, like the first time Ramoth flies to mate and Lessa discovers what nobody told her—that the riders of the dragons, telepathically tied to their mounts, also couple.

As mentioned before, a *pirn* is a kind of spool, or bobbin, used in weaving. McCaffrey uses extensive weaving imagery in *Dragonflight*. Most obviously, the mycorrhyzoid spore that propagates across vacuum from the Red Star to menace life on Pern is called Thread—metaphorically the stuff of which Pernese history is woven—an enemy, but one that stimulates cultural evolution. Further, Lytol, an ex-dragonrider and F'lar's chief informant on Search, is a weaver. Much is made of Lessa's clothing as she abandons her "drudge" disguise. She wears a special robe to the Hatching, as do all candidates for Impression. But most important, the clue to the

Riddle Song comes from a tapestry, which ultimately sends Lessa on her unprecedented journey *between* times to bring the Oldtimers forward. The tapestry has considerable significance in the novel—it is described in some detail, it aids in the development of flame-throwers, it is praised from an artistic standpoint, and ultimately it solves the problem of too few dragonriders to fight Thread. Lessa's voyage through time is the act that has the greatest impact on Pern's history in the entire dragon series.

None of this is to imply a direct one-to-one relationship between events on Pern and Yeats's cosmology. McCaffrey borrows extensively from Yeats for imagery to create a more powerful statement about imaginary history, but she is not following Yeats slavishly. So with most of McCaffrey's imagery. She does not use allegory; she borrows strong pictures from poetry, folklore, and the arts generally to increase the emotional impact of her story.

Admittedly, dragons in McCaffrey are much more than symbol. It is impossible to read the passages on the Impression of Ramoth or Ruth, or on the rising of Ramoth, or on the deaths of Wirenth and Prideth without buying totally into the reality of the dragons. Their world is so completely detailed, and they represent wishes so deep in the human subconscious for flight and absolute love that to reduce them to mere symbol would be asinine. The dragons, more than anything else, represent *themselves,* powerful beasts who can fly, whose love is perfect, whose breath is flame, whose mating deeply arouses all who are near them. So revered are they among the humankind of Pern that it is rude to criticize a dragonrider; oaths are made upon the Shell of the first queen dragon, Faranth. The *-th* suffix, which seems to mean *dragon* (corresponding to the *-el* we put on angel names, meaning *of God*: Raphael, Gabriel, etc.), is not repeated in any other Pernese name except for the name of one very old Hold, Ruatha—where, perhaps, dragons originated.

McCaffrey dragons are more interesting because they have five different forms: two types of female—gold and green; and three types of male—bronze, brown, and blue. In zoology, this variety of form is called *polymorphism.* A similar, if somewhat simpler, plan occurs with the lowly bee, which has both a fertile and an infertile female. McCaffrey's gold dragons may, upon mating, yield all five forms, but apparently the green female, if fertile at all, will produce only more greens. The dragon's mating pattern is not exactly copied from any terrestrial creature. Though insects and bats do mate in flight, the idea that the female attempts to evade the male's embrace, a pattern that ensures the reproduction of the strongest fliers, is not copied from terrestrial, winged-animal behavior.

The same caveat is necessary as preface to the discussion of dragons and the horse-and-rider image. Dragons and fire lizards represent the artistic vocation, the imaginative gift, and art itself, but they also have plot functions that are *not* connected with art. In other words, McCaffrey uses symbolism, not allegory.

To begin our discussion of dragons, just as the name of the planet Pern is taken from Yeats's mythos, the sun of Pern is related to dragons. In

Richard Hinckley Allen's *Star Names*, Rukbat is identified as Alpha Sagittarii, the Archer's Knee. More to the point, it was part of a larger Chinese zodiacal division called the Azure Dragon.[3]

McCaffrey's dragons, unlike the ferocious person-eating Celtic dragons, the one in *Beowulf*, or the dragons of Christian iconography, are not malevolent. About the only things she seems to have borrowed from Western dragon lore are the dragon's origin as a sea creature (hence fire lizards hatch on beaches) and the dragon's ability to breathe fire (although she invents an elaborate science-fictional explanation for this phenomenon: chewing and swallowing of a phosphine-bearing rock, which allows the dragon to belch forth burning gases). Rosemarie Arbur reduces to absurdity the theory that these traditional sources might be the inspiration for Pernese dragons by showing that the dragons would then be Tempters rather than friends and allies.[4] Oriental dragons are a bit less malevolent, but in their godlike power, they can scarcely be envisioned as telepathically linked to human riders. In fact, the more research one does on dragons, the less evidence there is that McCaffrey used any traditional model to create her dragons. If her dragons resemble anything out of classical literature, it might be Plato's image of the soul as a chariot drawn by winged horses in the *Phaedrus*. Hence we can think of dragons in terms of an image that pervades McCaffrey's work, which I call the horse-and-rider image and which probably has at least one source in McCaffrey's own love of horses and riding.

Fans interest themselves in whether animals as large as dragons can actually fly. McCaffrey finally cut off this line of inquiry by professing that Pernese dragons fly with the aid of psychokinesis. The dragons are warm-blooded, and their ability to belch flammable gas is apparently roughly analogous to the defense mechanism of the terrestrial bombardier beetle. Fire lizards—miniature dragons from which the dragons were bred up to size by the original Pern colonists—have every ability of the large dragons except for flaming. Though not as intelligent as dragons, they are more intelligent than any terrestrial subhuman species.

Draconic abilities to fly *between*, to communicate telepathically, and to travel through time are of course not based on terrestrial models, but McCaffrey considers these abilities natural faculties, which exist in embryonic form in humans waiting only for development. She does not consider them "magic" or supernatural.

On a symbolic level, however, dragons represent a spiritual dimension that echoes other images of flight in literature and mythology. McCaffrey, herself susceptible to the contagious excitement of dream-flight, translates the desire into the image of a horse and its rider. We see how the horse-and-rider image functions in *The Ship Who Sang*: Helva, the artist, is the controlling intelligence in a huge, powerful, beautiful starship that ultimately represents artistic imagination itself, the adventure of exploring inner space metaphorically represented by the adventure of exploring outer space. The same image is invoked in the title of the book *To Ride Pegasus*. The image is not a private one to McCaffrey; it is invoked in Peter Shaffer's *Equus* and in Plato's dialogue of love and rhetoric, the

Phaedrus. Its universality is demonstrated by the ecstasy children get from fast bicycles, cars, airplanes, and horses. In McCaffrey's personal life, it translated into a life-long desire for a horse, which finally resulted in her acquisition of Mr. Ed, who pleased her so much that she dedicated her gothic, *The Kilternan Legacy*, "to my Irish 'fairy' godmother, Hilda Whitton, who made my fondest wish come true in Mr. Ed." Even Yeats, from whom McCaffrey borrowed much Pernese imagery, has a horse-and-rider image in the dolphins who carry travelers across a "gong-tormented sea" in the poem "Byzantium" and in his self-proclaimed epitaph in "Under Ben Bulber," "Horseman pass by."

What then does the mount, in this case the dragon, represent? It is not art alone, surely, for the dragonriders Lessa, F'lar, F'nor, and Jaxom may be a number of things, including murderers and politicians, but seemingly not artists. Yet on a metaphoric level, they *are* artists; Lessa's psychic "pushing" (*DF* 44, for example) shapes the reality of the novel; she is the plot-mover, the stage manager of Pern. Whether tempers need to be soothed or tyrants need to be murdered, Lessa's gift is to influence events and thoughts to gain her ends. Thus does she ruin Ruatha Hold. Thus does she manipulate F'lar into a knife duel he never meant to fight, contrary to his honor, his mission, and his better judgment. Lessa is an artist in minds and in blood, a kind of psychic Lady Macbeth. F'lar, F'lon, Jaxom, Kylara, and T'ron, too, write history through their deeds, though none of them has Lessa's coercive psychic gift.

The dragons surely represent the intuitive side of the rider, the emotional, impulsive nature. Dragons make the final decisions about political leadership on Pern; a Hatchling chooses one girl from many to be her weyrmate, and that woman is the Weyr's co-leader. The adult queen dragon mates in a blood frenzy, baiting and jeering at her bronze suitors. Her caprice, sheer accident, or the brute power of the bronze determines which rider will be the Weyrwoman's mate. Much depends upon courage, strength, boldness, even humor and imagination, in the dragon's choice. Democracy plays only a small role, in that the sentiments of a Weyr can influence a mating flight, or a Weyr can close a flight to any but a favored bronze. But none can influence the choice of Hatchlings, as demonstrated in "The Smallest Dragonboy," when a bronze dragonet rejects all candidates presented in favor of a small boy with a broken leg who comes too late for the Hatching or, in the case of Mirrim and Path, when a green dragonet rejects presented males for an ineligible girl. "The dragons confer honor where *they* will," says F'lar (*DF* 66). When Ramoth first arises to mate, Lessa expresses the relationship thus: "Dragon instinct was limited to here-and-now, with no ability to control or anticipate. Mankind existed in partnership with them, to supply wisdom and order" (*DF* 133). The dragons mirror their riders' characters and emotions; thus the aphorism: "A dragon is no better than his rider" (*WD* 54). The emotional tone goes both ways, and many a rider is soothed by the comfortable thoughts of his adoring dragon.

But dragons are linked specifically with artistic activity in the Pern books. In *Dragonsong,* when Menolly believes she has lost her music, that she will never play her master's *gitar* again, her loss is expressed thus: "She knew now what a dragonless rider must feel" (*Dsong* 49). When she discovers the pleasure of playing a complex quartet with Domick, Sebell, and Talmor, she repeats the phrase "joy in music" to herself, knowing that it expresses her artistic delight. She remarks further, "I felt as if I was . . . was flying on a dragon!" (*Dsinger* 123).

Menolly, of course, cannot be a dragonrider. But the symbolism of dragons is miniaturized in the fire lizards, creatures with so much reader appeal that science-fiction conventions are crowded with people sporting small *stuffed* fire lizards on their shoulders. The fire lizards are taught to sing in harmony to Menolly, and she has nine of them, a number that seems significant since the queen of her group is called Beauty and since there are *nine* Muses. Much could also be made of the fact that Menolly's name (which sounds a bit like Melody) is similar in sound to *Mnemosyne,* the Greek goddess of memory and mother of the nine Muses. The fact that McCaffrey associates the name with a kind doctor from her past does not negate this possibility. Harpers, the leaders of the arts on Pern, impress fire lizards very easily; Robinton and Sebell both get one, and Piemur, interestingly, steals his queen egg from one of *nine* pots.

The nine-Muse motif is reflected in the dragons themselves, however, in the name of F'lar's dragon Mnementh, whose name is even more like *Mnemosyne,* with the draconic suffix -*th.* Yes, F'lar also is associated with memory, since it is he who understands and upholds the ancient traditions. But consider that an artwork, the tapestry of Ruatha Hold, sends Lessa on her 400-year errand *between,* thus saving human civilization on Pern. And an artwork, the Riddle Song, gives F'lar and Lessa the clues to know how to use the information in the tapestry. Lessa herself often resembles an artwork, a statuette (*DF* 106) or an icon with an aureole of hair, perhaps like the saints "in the gold mosaic of a wall" in Yeats's "Sailing to Byzantium."

Consider finally that the dragons' "jewel-faceted eyes" are more suggestive of art objects than of organic beings. The two largest types of dragon are the colors of gold and bronze, metals from which art objects are often made, and another color, blue, is the color favored by Harpers on Pern. The fire lizards, ancestors of the dragons, remind me of Yeats's "form as Grecian goldsmiths make/Of hammered gold and gold enamelling/To . . . set upon a golden bough to sing . . ." ("Sailing to Byzantium"). And after all, like the storyteller, balladeer, or scop, the dragons have the superhuman power to range through space and time—surely an artistic function!

None of the above is meant to reduce Pernese dragons (or fire lizards) to mere symbols of art. Dragons appeal to us on many levels, including the most childlike. They are immensely powerful, but their power is reined by the rider. They can fly, a dream so appealing to every human child and adult that a dream of flight, according to Patricia Garfield,[5] can enrapture the dreamer's heart. They have a homely dry humor. Hence, to undercut the sentimentality of a scene in which Lessa and F'lar look forward to the next mating flight as a draconic opportunity to consummate their human love, Ramoth comments laconically that F'lar's bronze might not be able to catch her in the mating flight (*DF* 214). Dragons endow the rider with enormous prestige. They are calm and gentle, almost maternal; yet in defense of their rider and other humans, they can produce flame—living pyrotechnics. They provide instant transportation from any point to any other point the rider or dragon can visualize. They are pets in docility and affection, but with wisdom and ability to communicate: an empathy so deep they read and transmit thoughts. Is it any wonder McCaffrey named Jaxom's dragon Ruth, after the daughter-in-law whose fidelity to her dead husband's mother finally brought both women to prosperity again? No wonder McCaffrey, in the dedication to *Dragonsong*, offered Beth Blish first place "in line for a dragon—behind me!"

But of all the human wishes dragons fulfill in fantasy, the deepest is the wish for perfect love. Rosemarie Arbur explores this aspect of dragon symbolism in her introduction to the McCaffrey bibliography. But in addition, the love-motif is connected to the sense of wonder because, beyond emotional and metaphysical implications of dragon love, is the scientific principle of imprinting. Any human love is based on insecurity, because it is conditional. Dragon love is unconditional because it is based on primitive, absolute, bonding-like imprinting. Even the shallow, selfish Kylara commands the absolute loyalty of her dragon Prideth. A dragon does not outlive its rider but flies *between* to death when its rider dies. Though psychology recently has made more of human bonding (as with Dorothy Tennov's study of romantic love, or "limerence," which she compares to the mating of birds in its exclusiveness, irrationality, and obsessiveness[6] and the discovery that bonding with infants appears most strongly when the adult is exposed to the infant immediately after birth), no human bonding is so invincible as the bond McCaffrey depicts between dragon and rider. What McCaffrey names *Impression* parallels the imprinting that occurs with birds and other creatures shortly after birth. But because it is biologically determined and absolute, the partners are free of the fear that they will be abandoned. Traditional views of romantic infatuation and love depict lovers as treacherous, unreliable, and sick with fantasy. So they are portrayed in Lysias's speech or Socrates' first speech in the *Phaedrus*.[7] This ugly portrayal of biologically determined, irrational love has survived the centuries to appear in the work of Abraham Maslow and George R. Bach. However, Socrates in the *Phaedrus* recants his original speech and develops the image of the soul as being in a chariot drawn by a good and bad horse, the ultimate function of which is to carry the soul toward heaven. And the beginning of the growth of the soul's wings occurs only when the soul begins to fall into the divine madness that Socrates recognizes as romantic love. The end of the flight is a reunion with the Ideal. This attitude toward love has been taken in modern times by such writers as Erich Fromm and Leo Buscaglia—instead of degrading the person or being a symptom of a maladjustment, the madness of love makes the person more alive, more sensitive, more giving, nearer to the divine.

McCaffrey apparently agrees with Plato, Fromm, and Buscaglia, because the children whom the dragons choose must have fine mettle—they must be imaginative, spirited, generous, just. And the relationship with the dragon ennobles them to the point where the dragonriders are the most respected people of Pern. Lessa's impatient vengeful streak is tempered by Ramoth; Mirrim's bitchiness improves after Impression; F'nor and Jaxom are supported by their dragons to the extent that F'nor would never have discovered fire lizards without Canth.

Of course, the bond between Pernese dragon and rider is not exactly like Dorothy Tennov's limerence, or Plato's divine madness, or Fromm's and Buscaglia's vision of human love, anymore than it is exactly like the bond between mother and baby or between a duckling and the object on which the duckling imprints. But this is exactly the advantage of treating such ideas in fiction—McCaffrey has stimulated our sense of wonder by suggesting similarities among these different types of love-bonding by portraying a wholly new type of bond that exists only in imagination in the form of Impression—the bond between dragon and rider—a marvelous achievement. Here is science fiction at its best, fictionalized intellectual history, the exploration of new ideas in new permutations to encourage wonder.

And not only do the Pernese dragons suggest perfect love made biological fact; they incorporate art, dreams of flight, power, generation of new life, perfect understanding, ethical improvement, and even spiritual elevation. No wonder they are such a captivating image!

Now let us turn to the structure of the two trilogies, *The Dragonriders of Pern* and the Harper Hall trilogy. Each trilogy is structurally independent; indeed, each individual novel is structurally independent, but the trilogies considered separately and in parallel show interesting structural features. Use of aphorisms, oaths, and stock similes, like Homeric epithets, unify all the Pern fiction. A list of the commonest oaths is given in the *Dragondex* in later editions of the adult trilogy; in addition, we have such sayings as "You've courage enough to fly with" (*DF* 59); "Each egg hatches a different way, but a crack at the right time speeds things up" (*DQ* 67); "A dragon is no better than his rider" (*WD* 54); "A face as long as a wet Turn" (*Dsong* 167); "My glow's not dim" (*Dsinger* 242); and "There are more ways of skinning a herdbeast than shaving him with a tableknife" (*DD* 29).[8] The ballads, too, provide a unifying element throughout the six volumes.

Individually, the volumes show McCaffrey's skill in using variety to maintain interest. Hence, incidents of love and romance alternate with incidents of adventure; incidents involving personal antagonisms alternate with speculation about scientific matters; knife fights alternate with intricate discussions of political hegemony; discovery alternates with incidents of ill health. For example, in chapter XIV of *The White Dragon*, Robinton is seen making a wager on the outcome of a mating flight—a touch of domestic humor. Then the exiled Southern riders join the mating flight—showing personal antagonism. Then there is a knife fight between F'lar and T'kul. Then Robinton has a heart attack—an outcome that has been hinted at throughout the chapter and that is linked to animosity about the mating flight. Finally, to round the chapter out, there is a reference to Robinton's wager on the mating flight, and the outcome of two conflicts—the wager and the flight itself—is revealed to end the suspense of the chapter. Moreover, the fact that Robinton relaxes, knowing the outcome, resolves the suspense over whether he will survive the heart attack. So, essentially, in this neatly crafted chapter, we have had four conflicts, all interwoven causally, each resolved at the end of the chapter. Nor is this type of structural excellence limited to individual chapters. Lessa's premonition at the beginning of *Dragonflight* is never fully explained until part III, when she realizes that the premonition was caused by her own time-traveling presence, dragon-mounted in the sky (*DF* 188). And the "discrepant portents" never are fully explained—or combated—until the end of the novel when Lessa has brought forward the lost Weyrs and, with their help, the dragons fight Thread successfully. McCaffrey's fine sense of plotting instructs her to create variety through alternating types of conflict and unity through setting conflict early and resolving it at the end, often with more than one conflict resolved through the same incident.

Relationships between *The Dragonriders of Pern* and the Harper Hall trilogy show parallels and contrasts that form a counterpoint pattern, like Domick's contrapuntal music that so entrances Menolly (*Dsinger* 123). The elements in the "adult" trilogy (*Dragonflight, Dragonquest,* and *The White Dragon*) are miniaturized in the juvenile trilogy. The characters in the adult trilogy are older than Menolly and Piemur. Lessa is about twenty at the beginning of *Dragonflight* and is verging on middle age in *The White Dragon.* Menolly is about fourteen at the beginning of *Dragonsong* and is only blossoming into womanhood at the end of *Dragondrums.* Jaxom, the leading figure in the last novel of the adult series, *The White Dragon,* declares his adult status at the beginning of that novel and is confirmed as Lord Holder, a sign of his majority, at the end. Piemur, the other major figure in the juvenile series, is about ten at the beginning and only about fourteen at the end.

The period of time encompassed by the adult series is also longer than that of the juvenile series. The adult series starts shortly before the Present Pass and ends in the fifteenth year of the Pass, a period of seventeen or eighteen years. The juvenile series starts in the seventh Turn of the Present Pass and ends about the twelfth Turn—a period of no more than five years. The very length of the novels in each series reflects the lighter, "miniaturized" nature of the juvenile series—a total of only 706 pages versus 1,135 in the adult.

The fire lizards, the dominant alien life form in the juvenile series, are miniatures of the dragons. Their hatching, impression, and flights *between* imitate the grander corresponding events in the lives of dragons and provide a glimpse of Weyr-life in miniature for non-dragonriders. The fire lizards are even more surely a symbol for the elevation of the human soul than the larger beasts. Thus Robinton, having impressed the fire lizard Zair, says: "I have stood so long peering through a small opening into another Hold of understanding. Now I can see without obstruction" (*Dsinger* 174), echoing St. Paul's description of divine grace, "For now we see through a glass darkly; but then face to face" (I Corinthians 13:12).

McCaffrey arouses our sense of wonder in a large, epic way by the Impression and mating of dragons and in a small, lyric way by fire lizards pulling Menolly out of the ocean by her hair (*DD* 233) or fetching her pipes (*Dsinger* 101). Even the punctuation reflects the big-little relationship— *Impression, Hatching, Egg,* are words capitalized in reference to dragons, but not to fire lizards.

The ballads of Pern, too, reflect the big-little relationship of the adult and juvenile trilogies, most particularly "Moreta's Ride" and Menolly's "Fire Lizard Song." Joanne Forman has created music for some of McCaffrey's dragon and fire lizard ballads,[9] and a full article could be devoted to their function in the dragon books. "Moreta's Ride" is first alluded to in *Dragonflight* (*DF* 20, 99, 305) and then described (though not quoted) in *Dragonsinger* (*Dsinger* 131-132). It describes the tragic exploit of a woman mounted on a dragon. "Fire Lizard Song" is quoted at the beginning of *Dragonsinger* and concerns a man saving a clutch of fire lizards. The subject matter of "Moreta's Ride" is also much lengthier. At any rate, a full book, *Moreta, Dragonlady of Pern,* expands the legend. Interestingly, there is a sex-role reversal in both pieces; Piemur sings the part of Moreta in "Moreta's Ride" while Menolly transforms the Holder in "Fire Lizard Song" from a girl (herself) to an anonymous male.

More generally, McCaffrey's interest in miniatures and big-little relationships is highlighted when Mnementh, to please F'lar, catches Lessa to prevent her fleeing (*DF* 59) and cages her in his huge talons—as Menolly does later with hatching fire lizards (*Dsong* 84).

Parallels in structure are also reflected in the leading characters in the trilogies. The first book of each trilogy deals with a young woman, a Cinderella figure. Lessa is a ragged drudge who is carried away by a princely man, F'lar. She is given new clothes, then meets her "fairy godmother"—the dragon Ramoth—reversing the order of the fairy tale. Menolly, also like Cinderella, is mistreated by her own parents after the death of her spiritual father, Petiron. She, too, is carried away by a man on a dragon and taken to the palace-like Weyr. Recalling Cinderella, Menolly loses both shoes in her flight. She is also given new clothes by a kindly "fairy godmother," Felena, and a second set by Silvina. Both young women subsequently become something akin to royalty on Pern: Lessa becomes Weyrwoman and Menolly becomes apprentice to the Masterharper. Both women Impress queens—Lessa a golden dragon and Menolly a golden fire lizard. Both women are resourceful and independent and are capable of surviving without human company or support in isolation. Both are highly empathic and bond to animals easily. Both women have impact on Pern's history: Lessa by bringing forward the lost Weyrs and Menolly by artistic genius and knowledge of fire lizards. Both women shatter sex stereotypes: Lessa by flying and fighting Thread and Menolly by becoming a musician. McCaffrey has reversed the big-little relationship here; Lessa is petite and Menolly is so well grown that she is mistaken for a boy.

Both women also pass through serious illness on their way to greatness, which nearly prevents them from accomplishing their goals: Lessa's ill ness from going backward in time 400 years almost prevents her from rousing the lost Weyrs to follow her forward, and Menolly's delirium from packtail poisoning nearly costs her the use of her hand to play *gitar*. Both women are persecuted by father figures: Lessa by Fax, and Menolly by her own father, Yanus. Both, finally, are ugly ducklings who emerge into beauty and grace as they leave their unappreciative families and homes and travel to new places.

The final novel of each trilogy is dominated by a male figure, Jaxom and Piemur. Both boys are required to show their adulthood by keeping secrets: Jaxom, the secret that he, not an Oldtimer, returned the stolen queen dragon Egg; Piemur, all the secrets he hears on the drum heights, plus the fact that he is Robinton's agent and all the secrets he learns while serving Robinton. Both boys eventually show their maturity to a male mentor, Lytol and Robinton, respectively, and obtain confirmation of their adult status at the end of each novel: Jaxom by being Confirmed as Lord Holder of Ruatha and Piemur by becoming drum-journeyman. Like the two women, each young man goes through a trial by illness: Jaxom when he gets fire-head and Piemur when his fellow students grease the steps and he falls downstairs, injuring his head. Like the two women, the young men are both empathic with animals, particularly Piemur, who rescues a small runnerbeast. There are a number of parallels between Piemur and Menolly: they both are persecuted by jealous peers; they both survive outside civilization—a kind of rite of passage like the Eagle Scout ordeal—and endure Thread-fall outside a Hold; they both impress fire lizards in the wilderness; they both find a dying animal to feed and oil their fire lizards; and they both are promoted to journeyman at the conclusion of their adventures.

However, the most interesting parallelism and interweaving of plots and subplots involve the egg motif. Both Jaxom and Piemur succeed in Impressing against the expectations of their elders: Jaxom Impressing Ruth and Piemur impressing the stolen fire-lizard egg. Both Impressions underscore the irrevocability of Impression: Jaxom is not separated from Ruth, and Piemur is never even scolded for stealing Farli's egg. The major exploit of each boy is also an egg *theft*—Piemur's theft of his fire-lizard egg and Jaxom's much more dangerous theft—or rather return—of the stolen queen dragon Egg, an exploit that prevents planetary war on Pern.

Jaxom's exploits are an epic version of Piemur's picaresque adventures, and they deserve one or two other observations. Jaxom's name is two letters different from *Jason*, just as Lessa's is two letters off from *Leda*. Like Jason in mythology, Jaxom is called upon to steal something or rather steal it back: Jason was to obtain the Golden Fleece, Jaxom a golden Egg. Jaxom, like Jason, becomes involved with a woman whom he uses to his own ends with no real love—Corana, in *The White Dragon*, corresponds to Medea—although without the sorcery or revenge motif. Just as Jason eventually rejects Medea for Creusa, princess of Corinth, Jaxom rejects Corana for Sharra, sister of a Lord Holder—politically desirable marriages to high-born ladies. McCaffrey seems to have chosen

Jaxom's name based on dragons in the Jason legend: Medea's chariot was in the shape of a dragon, and one of Jason's trials was to sow a field with dragon's teeth.

The Pern books are unmistakably both feminine and feminist. Harlan Ellison, in an essay on *Dragonflight,* concludes, "There are all too few guerrilla warriors in the jungle these days. If McCaffrey can keep from getting her skirts caught in the underbrush, she may be our next Che Guevara."[10] Ellison claims that the novel "fails in parts . . . to which the female orientation has been brought, and applied."[11] However, when he comes to specifics (and Ellison is nothing if not a superior editor and teacher), he attacks mainly tics of diction that echo gothic romance, tidbits like "teasing vexatiousness." He points out virtually nothing in the *plot* of the novel that weakens it by being female in orientation. Specifically, McCaffrey uses a lot of hard science-fiction concepts (mycorrhyzoid spores, breeding of fire lizards, astronomy, etc.) and writes scenes of physical combat comparable to those written by men. Particularly exciting are F'lar's knife fights with Fax, T'ron, and T'kul—one in each book of the adult trilogy. No one has ever claimed writers can't write combat scenes because they lack personal experience; in fact, how many *male* science-fiction writers regularly engage in street fights? In modern society, male and female experience of the world is not that different, and where it is, McCaffrey has an edge by her ability to see events through the "minority" female viewpoint. Neither femininity nor feminism damages the Pern books.

And the Pern books show evidence of a feminist point of view—if we remember that they are about a renaissance. Pre-renaissance culture on Pern is quite sexist; the renaissance brings equality and opportunity for women.

Pernese domestic life, to begin with, is markedly sexist. Marleen Barr's perceptive essay on Menolly demonstrates the cruel repression of a young woman's talent.[12] Drudges shown in the Holds and Halls are mostly female, though late in *The White Dragon* a specifically male drudge is alluded to (*WD* 237). Women do not rule Holds; their political power in the Holds is expressed only through marriage, though Lessa does try to claim power in Ruatha after F'lar kills Fax. The episode in *Dragonquest* where F'lar and Lessa visit the Mastersmith's Crafthall in Telgar Hold shows interplay of attitudes toward women's role. F'lar observing that the women serve food without demanding attention (there are no craftswomen), teases Lessa by telling Fandarel, "I see you've got your women trained" (*DQ* 132). Necessity has forced the craftsmen to draft women to do menial craft work—a step up from cooking and scrubbing, but still not creative scientific work. Lessa imports a group of women to fill in as housewives and nurturers for the craftsmen.

McCaffrey is not necessarily implying that women are fit only to cook, clean, and kowtow. There seems to be recognition of the dignity of housekeeping chores. Cooking itself is regarded as an art worth learning. But labor in the Weyrs is divided along sexual lines. Lessa and Manora are responsible for the management of the Weyr household, though Lessa is also brought in on policy decisions. On one occasion, however, F'lar excludes her from a policy decision, when F'nor has been wounded by T'reb (*DQ* 24). Men in the Weyr, in contrast, take care of their dragons and fight Thread. The Weyrs do allow more freedom and power for women than the Holds and Crafts, however. In the Holds, women are not even expected to be able to read (*DF* 115).

Naming on Pern is curiously nonsexist. Women do not take their husbands' names, nor is the child given the father's name. Instead, a name is constructed out of sounds from both the father's and mother's names. For example, Felessan is the son of F'lar and Lessa. The natural order on Pern also has elements of feminine supremacy; gold dragons, the females, are bigger than their bronze mates. A gold can outfly all but one of the other dragons in her Weyr—the bronze that becomes her mate. In other words, the female dragon gets a wide choice of mates and selects the best through a contest. This process is part of a motif found elsewhere in McCaffrey, which I call the Atalanta motif. Atalanta, in mythology, had been warned that her marriage was to bring her unhappiness. So she announced that she would marry only the man who won a race with her. Suitors who lost would forfeit their lives. Hippomenes tricked her by dropping golden apples in her path. Gold dragons reenact this contest, though suitors are not slain—except for Salth who bursts his heart pursuing Caylith (*WD* 280).

But the Pern books are about a renaissance. A woman, Mirrim, Impresses Path, a green dragon. Nature seems to be telling humans that animal nature encourages equality—indeed, green dragons are female, and McCaffrey hints that the telepathic tie riders have with their dragons requires that when the green dragon flies to mate, her rider, who is except for Mirrim always male, is impelled to engage in homosexual intercourse with the rider of the dragon who flies her. Jaxom, for one, is uncomfortable with this arrangement and is rather relieved when Ruth, his dragon, proves to be asexual.

A symbolic hint that sex roles are going to change occurs when F'lar and Lessa twice enact an "Adam and Eve" scene in which one offers the other a piece of fruit (*DF* 83–84 and *DF* 260). In the second case, the Biblical parallel is archly highlighted with F'lar's words, "Let us eat and die together!" In both cases, the fruit is introduced simultaneously with new knowledge: first, with the knowledge that Pern is going to have a new Weyrwoman and second, with the knowledge that the Southern Continent is habitable. In fact, there is a "serpent" involved in both cases—a dragon in the first and grub in the second. But the reference is ironic because the knowledge in these cases is good, and—most tellingly—the *man* offers the fruit to the *woman*, a reversal of the conventional anti-feminist version where woman is blamed for tempting man to sin.

Women in McCaffrey, in any case, are seldom reduced to passive, hand-wringing objects of pity or rescue. Lessa is an independent sort who gave up all the joys of romance and pretty clothes to get revenge on the man who murdered her family. Although it occurs to her when she goes to Benden in *Dragonflight* that she might be forced to serve sexually a man in the Weyr, this possibility is dismissed with neither delight nor horror. She's more interested in the prestige and political power F'lar has hinted she may receive. The romance element in F'lar's and Lessa's relationship is downplayed; F'lar isn't even sure she's attractive and in any case has nothing but contempt for "pretty" women, like Jora (*DF* 72). Romance, for both of them, takes a back seat to leadership of Pern's renaissance. She is more interested in male prerogatives like riding a dragon, fighting Thread, and saving Pern by being the first person to travel through time.

Lessa does have two feminine foibles: manipulativeness and secretiveness. She learns to control both of these failings; her attempts to get dragonriders to poach from the Holds leads to a premature breach in Weyr solidarity (*DF* 128), and she finds that concealing her ability to talk to all dragons deprives F'lar of a valuable strategic tool (*DF* 211). Her deviousness, ultimately, is used, like Robinton's, in Pern's defense, as when she sweet-talks T'ron out of valuable ancient records (*DQ* 52–53).

Ultimately, the peaceful transfer of the leadership of Ruatha to Jaxom—and by implication all the progress made in the dragon books—is attributed to Lessa. At the end of *The White Dragon,* F'lar says, "It's your day, too, Lessa . . . A day your determination and spirit made possible!" (*WD* 472). F'lar's achievements are physical and political: knife fights, trading of land, encouraging science. Lessa is also political, but her deeds are worthy of being made into a ballad: Domick's composition about her time-travel mission (*WD* 7). She transcends mere politics; she is the guiding spirit of progress; she changes Pern's history.

Menolly likewise is no mere pawn of male dominance. Marleen Barr's feminist analysis of *Dragonsong* emphasizes the sexism of Menolly's family and Hold;[13] Menolly herself, however, is a person of extraordinary character and achievement. Her virtues are more than emotional and mental; a physically powerful woman, she outruns the leading edge of Thread and offers to fight a duel over an insult. There are two feminist ironies in *Dragonsong* and its two sequels: first, McCaffrey introduces the new Harper Elgion so coyly that everybody, including the reader, expects him to be the center of a romance. The reader rather hopes Menolly will pair off with him—after all, the abused girl deserves something nice. But Menolly is made of far finer stuff, and her triumph is not to be romantic, but vocational. Adornment and romance interest her far less than artistic self-expression. At the end of *Dragonsong,* we rejoice that she will have music—not that she will degenerate into a happy bride. Menolly does have a love interest later, but not at the expense of her music.

The other irony is the sexist treatment of music on Pern. McCaffrey of all people must have delighted in the ineptness of assuming that women could not be musicians since McCaffrey herself is both a professional singer and director. The horrible effects of sexism are shown not just in the fact that a female role in a ballad has to be sung by a little boy, but in the devastating effects on women musicians in general. Pona, Audiva, Briala, and Amania are all incompetent, either because their talents have been misdirected or because they have grown up with the expectation that they, as females, are incapable of making music (*Dsinger* 87). As disagreeable as they may seem (the name *Amania* is only one letter off from the name of a poisonous mushroom, *amanita*), their fates seem unfair. If Menolly can be such a fine musician, could it be partially because her teacher, Petiron, has *expected* her to do well? Silvina, too, is a good musician (*Dsinger* 158). There is a hint that the exclusion of the girls from impromptu music may be a factor (*Dsinger* 134). Cultural factors must be at work here; *we* know that musical talent is not sexually determined. But we are not from Pern.

Interestingly, the stupid and evil people of Pern are those who buy into the traditional stereotypes of women. Fax, for example, can think of no greater insult than to call F'lar and F'lon "dragonwomen" (*DF* 53). Meron (whose name irresistibly echoes *moron*) uses "weyrwoman" in a similarly insulting tone to Lessa (*DQ* 251) and demonstrates his manhood by leaving bruises on his sex partner, Kylara (*DQ* 62), as well as being surly and aggressive on many occasions. Kylara is also a stereotypical female—almost a parody of Scarlett O'Hara—a "southern belle" from Southern Weyr, interested in finery more than good manners, who practices her wiles upon every man (including F'nor, and even F'lar), who misuses her nurse servant, Rannelly, and whose maxim is "A frown is a mighty weapon . . . but do cultivate a pretty one" (*DQ* 61). The sexist attitudes of all these characters get them in trouble: Fax's taunting leads to a fatal knife fight, and Meron's sexual prowess and Kylara's careless exploitation of her prettiness lead to the death of her dragon. There is even a hint that Meron's irregular sexual appetites—we assume that he's sadistic from Kylara's bruises—end with poetic justice in his wasting disease in *Dragondrums* (*DQ* 63, *DD* 122, 165).

Unquestionably, McCaffrey endorses free expression of women's talent and rejects many archaic sex-role stereotypes. However, Pern is not a society in which full equality is possible. Women are nurturers and facilitators. They manipulate rather than control through outright power. At the same time, the nurturant and manipulative role is given full dignity. There are an astonishing number of references to food and drink in the series. Whenever someone needs to be saved, healed, rescued, reassured, impressed, thanked, influenced, supported, or bedded, there is food—whether it be hot klah, good Benden wine to get Robinton to swallow medicine for his heart attack, or stew to assure Menolly that she's safe from Thread. Bad food is a disgrace and a warning—so with Fax's disastrous visit to Ruatha (*DF* 42). Good food is evidence of thrift, good deeds, and industry—so with Lessa and F'lar's visit to the Telgar Crafthall when Lessa sends more cooks to improve the craftsmen's lifestyle (*DQ* 136).

Good women in the dragon books are good cooks and good housekeepers; bad women are bad cooks and sloppy housekeepers. The nurturant role for women is inescapable. Men are more likely to show love through other means; F'lar, when Lessa returns from her time-journey, shows his intense relief first by shaking her and then later through sex. F'nor reacts to Brekke's tragedy by watching continuously at her bedside. Jaxom demonstrates his love for Sharra by daringly snatching her from her brother's Hold. Much of this stereotypical attitude toward love and feeding—women show love by feeding, men show love by sex and action—is rooted in the role food has in Impression. After a fire lizard or a dragon has been Impressed, it turns to its impressor for feeding. Food is the stuff of bonding, and women are in charge of food. Bonding is primarily a feminine function, though of course it occurs with creatures of both sexes. Food is love; women provide food. If there is any sexist stereotyping inherent in the social structure of Pern, this is the emotional basis of it, and Pern's renaissance cannot change it. Nor, in McCaffrey's world, should it change.

McCaffrey's achievement in the dragon books is impressive. Using powerful symbolic allusions, she depicts a society undergoing a renaissance. Her themes of esthetic transcendence and bonding are underscored through a strong poetic metaphor of winged dragons, a parallel to the horse-and-rider motif elsewhere in her work. Plot and characterization interrelate to these symbols and themes. The structure of each book and the structure of each trilogy show intricate counterpointing of plot, character, and symbol, with subtle use of scale (big-little) as a patterning element. The books show realistic treatment of women as dignified and interesting characters, not mere stick figures existing as foils to the male characters.

Nor has my discussion exhausted literary analysis of the dragon books. The relationship of the seventh volume, *Moreta, Dragonlady of Pern*, to the intricate patterning of plots is a topic for further investigation.

Set some nine hundred years before the events of *Dragonflight*, *Moreta, Dragonlady of Pern* (1983) is a radical departure from all of the previous dragon books. The events of the book are alluded to in *Dragonsinger* (*Dsinger* 131-132) and *Dragonflight* (*DF* 20, 99, 305), although the novel does not conform perfectly to "The Ballad of Moreta's Ride" as sung by the Masterharper's Hall and directed by Menolly. As described in *Dragonflight* (*DF* 99), going *between* does turn out to be a critical issue, since Moreta dies by not returning from *between*. But in *Dragonsinger*, the dying Moreta is borne *between* by her own dragon, Orlith. In *Moreta*, she dies on another queen dragon's back. In *Dragonsinger*, Moreta is the only rider well enough to deliver the cure. In *Moreta*, she is one of several riders and has been pressed into service because of the uncooperativeness of M'tani, Telgar Weyrleader. In *Dragonsinger*, the cure is seeds from Nabol and Ista. In *Moreta*, there is no cure, but there is a vaccine that is administered with hollow needlethorns from Ista and Nerat. Most interesting of all, Moreta is actually carrying not human, but runnerbeast, vaccine. Many of these discrepancies can be ascribed to minor errors in oral transmission over nine-hundred years and loss of relevant medical knowledge. The artistic advantage in basing the novel on material in previous novels is that the readers are aware that the sympathetic, likable heroine is going to die, but are in suspense as to exactly how and why.

If the plot, at least in broad strokes, is no surprise, there is plenty of novel characterization. McCaffrey creates over two hundred new characters (counting dragons but not counting named runnerbeasts and watch-whers). Among them are several striking portraits of women, including the wryly humorous Desdra; the affectionate Dalova; the strong, loyal Nerilka; and best of all, the spirited, acid-witted old lady, Leri. Leri is a special triumph because with her McCaffrey creates a portrait of a highly likable elderly woman—rare in science fiction.

Of the male characters, the irascible, strong, but somewhat stupid Sh'gall makes a memorable impression, as does the cynical but sentimental Capiam and the charming Harper Tuero, who, like Robinton, loves Benden wine but is less scrupulous in how he obtains it.

Most interesting is Alessan, who, though sexy and fun-loving at the beginning of the novel, has the courage to tend the sick and plow the fields of the Hold over which he is Lord. *Alessan* suggests that the naming custom of Pern often preserves for posterity a beloved name, for Lessa, nine hundred years later, must be his descendant.

The charming B'lerion, too, is a memorable character. His verve in pursuing special women (Moreta and Oklina) also extends to "timing it" with his dragon to collect needlethorn. His name echoes *Bellerophon,* the Greek hero who fought Chimaera with arrows from astride Pegasus, just as B'lerion fights the plague with needlethorn by riding his dragon. McCaffrey also alludes to her horse-and-rider image in a special way here, for Bellerophon's immortal mount was Pegasus, the winged horse.

There are also several sympathetic portraits of homosexual love, involving green dragon riders and their blue-rider lovers or, in one case, a healer.

The book also casts new light on Pern's past and on its flora and fauna. The Dragondex provides detailed information about dragon sizes and functions, along with information about the genetic manipulation that created both dragons and watch whers. Runnerbeasts are apparently related to horses, from Earth, as the rare feline that supposedly infects Pern with the plague is to cats. Details of dragon anatomy and Pernese pharmacopoeia are given, including the fact that dragons bleed green ichor and have more than one heart and also the hint that more on Pern was genetically manipulated than dragons—including perhaps needle-thorn, numbweed, fellis, and other useful plants. McCaffrey apparently did considerable research into medieval crafts and into surgical techniques, in addition.

Moreta, Dragonlady of Pern is that rare bird among McCaffrey's works, a tragedy of sorts. Only one other protagonist in her work dies—Killashandra. Yet Killashandra's death, in the last *Continuum* story, is the result of treachery, a tale of human evil. In Moreta's death, too, there is the hint of some treachery—M'tani's obstructionism—but mostly her death is an unexpected, untimely accident. If there is irony, it is an irony of broken plans. The book begins with Moreta deciding that she'll grow her hair long after the Pass is over (*MDP* 3)—but she never gets the chance. She wonders if Orlith's telepathic voice will acquire the depth of Holth's when Orlith is old (*MDP* 169)—but Orlith dies young. Leri tells Moreta that she has the *makings* of a fine Weyrwoman (*MDP* 235)—little realizing that within a day, Moreta will have earned a special ballad in her name—

in honor of her death. In the same passage, Leri suggests that Moreta find a new Weyrleader—little dreaming that, for Moreta, there will be no more lovers or weyrmates. The very morning of her death, Moreta makes plans to restock the Weyr, to Search for candidates, and to insist that Leri and her Holth move to a warmer climate (*MDP* 251, 252).

Yet death, in the context of the novel, is only a meaningless boundary. Moreta's life has been full and well lived. She has reveled in racing and loving. She has borne several children, conceived in full lust and passion. She does everything with verve—rides not just her own dragon, but others. She loves the equine runnerbeasts, a further allusion to the horse-and-rider motif. She is a woman not ashamed to perspire, whether from fighting Thread or dancing at a Gather (*MDP* 1, 3, 32). She is a brilliant veterinary surgeon. She has many warm friendships, among men as well as women. Not much more than a month before her death, she consummates an affair with a charismatic nobleman, Alessan. Most important, she is the rider of her own dragon, Orlith. The commonest things are exciting and zestful to Moreta. "I have seen the rainforest resemble a green face with a thousand dark-rimmed eyes," she says (*MDP* 216), speaking only of the mundane gathering of medicinal supplies. For Moreta, the world is charged with beauty and wonder.

Ultimately, the book is a celebration of the indomitable strength of human imagination. The inspiration for the plague vaccine itself comes from an imaginative work, a ballad. The phrase "it's in their blood," recited lyrically by Tirone, prompts Capiam to isolate the blood factor for the vaccine. Though Moreta dies, her tradition lives on in song, memory, and deed. The very day Orlith and Leri fly *between* to their death, Orlith's Eggs Hatch and the miraculous cycle of dragon-bonding begins again with Oklina's Impression of Hannath. Oklina is sister to Moreta's latest love, and lover to the father of Moreta's third child. It is as if Oklina is taking up Moreta's life and spirit. Moreta's death, caused by an error in flying *between*, is not an ordinary death, but a glorious one, available only to a woman who has soared as few humans have done.

Though the themes and settings of *Moreta, Dragonlady of Pern* are consonant with the two trilogies, this latest volume clearly represents a new direction in depicting McCaffrey's Pern. And it admits of sequels.

NOTES

[1] William Butler Yeats, *The Collected Poems of W. B. Yeats* (New York: Macmillan, 1956), pp. 184-185, 191-192, 211-212, 243-244.

[2] John Unterecker, *A Reader's Guide to William Butler Yeats* (New York: Noonday, 1959), pp. 25-29.

[3] Richard Hinckley Allen, *Star Names: Their Lore and Meaning* (New York: Dover, 1963), pp. 356-357.

[4] Rosemarie Arbur, *Leigh Brackett, Marion Zimmer Bradley, Anne McCaffrey: A Primary and Secondary Bibliography* (Boston: G. K. Hall, 1982), pp. xx-xxi. A more detailed treatment of dragon-lore may be found in Deborah Burros, "On Dragons," in *Pern Portfolio*, ed. A. E. Zeek (Staten Island, NY: Isis/Yggdrisil Press), pp. 18-27.

[5] *Creative Dreaming* (New York: Ballantine, 1976), pp. 133-142.

[6] Dorothy Tennov, *Love and Limerence: The Experience of Being in Love* (Briarcliff Manor, NY: Stein and Day, 1979), pp. 248–254.

[7] Plato, *Lysis, or Friendship; The Symposium; Phaedrus,* trans. and preface by Benjamin Jowett (New York: Heritage, 1968), pp. 146–159.

[8] Quotations adjusted to present tense.

[9] *Dragonsongbook* (Taos, NM: Performing Arts Press, c. 1983).

[10] *The Book of Ellison,* Ed. Andrew Porter (New York: Algol Press, 1978), p. 140.

[11] Ellison, 130.

[12] "Science Fiction and the Fact of Women's Repressed Creativity: Anne McCaffrey Portrays a Female Artist," *Extrapolation,* 23, No. 1 (Spring 1982), 70–76.

[13] Barr, 71.

V

TO RIDE PEGASUS AND *GET OFF THE UNICORN:*
Further Development of the Horse-and-Rider Motif

To Ride Pegasus (1973) and *Get Off the Unicorn* (1977) represent departures from McCaffrey's previous work and show the variety of styles and themes she can develop. *To Ride Pegasus,* following on the heels of books set in far-future worlds—*Dragonflight* (1968), *Decision at Doona* (1969), *The Ship Who Sang* (1969), and *Dragonquest* (1973)—seemed to surprise the critics, who expected and wanted novels from her based on technology and knowledge utterly beyond present-day experience. Parapsychology seemed too near normal experiences, and the setting of *To Ride Pegasus* seemed too near today's New Jersey and New York. Near-future settings, in the politically volatile early seventies, implied political judgments that were controversial. McCaffrey's treatment of crime and economic problems made some critics bristle, and her portrayal of women in a near-future world was not feminist enough for some and too feminist for others. Yet the book was and is very popular, and justly so.

Get Off the Unicorn treats many of the same themes as *To Ride Pegasus,* but the short-story format made clear that the setting of each story was only one possibility for a McCaffrey future, alternate, or present-day world. Together the two books explore the possibilities of the human psyche, both in terms of adapting to environment and in terms of evolving into *homo superior* through development of psychic gifts. They also show the variety of speculative premises McCaffrey can develop as well as evidence of narrative experimentation. The horse-and-rider image and the flight image pervade both books, showing McCaffrey's interest in the potential of human imagination.

Perhaps McCaffrey should be flattered that *To Ride Pegasus* provoked one of the most vituperative reviews in science-fiction criticism I, at least, have ever read—this from M. John Harrison, writing in *New Worlds* #6.[1] Harrison's attack has two prongs: first, the love scene between Ruth Horvath and her husband Lajos implies a "set of disgusting old wives' tales" suitable "for not even the mawkish of journals." Second, Harrison charges elitism: McCaffrey tags her psionic protagonists as above the rabble. The Talented are interested only in protecting the property of the "haves"; the "have-nots" are mere "dancing bears," regarded with "complete lack of compassion."

The first charge was not original. Sam Lundwall makes it, specifically about "A Womanly Talent," when he criticizes the scene where Daffyd

53

op Owen watches Ruth and Lajos's coital graph—and indeed, only McCaffrey could make a polygraph reading seem almost pornographic.[2] The needle recording Ruth's brain activity shows "frenetic action" from "excited and conflicting signals." Its transistors are "sensitive," like erogenous zones. The needle gouges "deeply . . . flinging its tip back and forth." The "final high" is "tight, intense." The polygraph itself seems to be experiencing orgasm. Daffyd op Owen and Welch are both, appropriately, a little embarrassed, even though what they are really seeing is not orgasm, but Ruth's psionic powers at work shaping the genes of the child to be conceived.

Susan Wood's apt defense of this scene is based on McCaffrey's own admission that John W. Campbell, who originally used the chapter as a story in *Analog,* had wanted Ruth defined in a traditional feminine role.[3] McCaffrey had the last laugh by making the feminine role not quite as passive as Campbell had in mind. Ruth does something no man can do—create a child to order—and she does it not just with her body, but with her mind.

Harrison's second attack is more serious. *To Ride Pegasus* is indeed an elitist book, but it is elitist in the same way much science fiction is. It posits the existence of a group of people who are an evolutionary development beyond humankind as we know it—*homo superior.* The ethical problem is how shall *homo superior* treat *homo sapiens*? McCaffrey is not the first writer to portray *homo superior* with this ethical problem. The theme is endemic to science fiction, perhaps because science-fiction readers themselves are possessed of a mild megalomania: they consider themselves superior in intelligence and imagination to the mass of mankind. Hence, the popularity of Olaf Stapledon's *Odd John* and A. E. van Vogt's *Slan.* Two issues recur: 1) the persecution of *homo superior* by *homo sapiens* and 2) the question of whether *homo superior* shall protect the life and happiness of *homo sapiens.* McCaffrey's treatment of these two issues, as with almost all her fiction, is more optimistic and benevolent than their treatment by other writers. In brief, she sees *homo superior* trading the benefits of superior mental powers (precognition, "finding," psychic healing, crime detection, etc.) for protection and power in the majority world of *homo sapiens,* solving both problems with one neat principle. Of course, *To Ride Pegasus* has an elitist bias: the protagonists are as much superior to humankind as we know it as humankind is to the Neanderthal.

These themes are elaborated in the book through the notion of humans evolving toward godhood with allusions to Pope's *An Essay on Man* and through flight imagery. This last is again related to McCaffrey's recurrent motif, the horse-and-rider image, this time with a winged horse.

McCaffrey's optimistic outlook permeates her fiction. The human ability to solve problems through reason with human feeling is a cornerstone of her philosophy. So it is natural that she sees humans as ever-improving, ever-evolving toward something more godlike. Not only will the future person—*homo superior*—be more intelligent, he and she will also be more loving, just, and ethical. The specific evolutionary development

McCaffrey sees as the most likely quantum jump between *homo sapiens* and *homo superior* is psychic ability. Specifically, she forecasts organic changes in the human brain that permit broadcast and receiving telepathy, similar powers of empathy, psychokinesis (or power to move objects through mental effort alone), precognition, psychic healing, and psychic finding of lost objects and persons. These ideas are treated in other short fiction, and they appear in the dragon books. For example, Lessa can communicate telepathically with her own and other dragons, and Moreta has a psychic healing gift. In *To Ride Pegasus,* McCaffrey theorizes on how these abilities might work. Specifically, she suggests that they may obey some kind of inverse-square rule, like electromagnetic radiation. Hence, the empath idiot Harold Orley becomes more wildly excited as he approaches his hysterical quarry, Solange Boshe. The psychic "radiation" passes through buildings, but there is some kind of shielding material that can stop it so that poor Harold is not constantly plagued by others' distresses. In the first chapter, McCaffrey also indicates that a special encephalogram can indicate the presence of psychic brain activity: the Goosegg.

As with any superior ability, those who possess it are generally average or superior in other realms, but there are those whose mind or personality has been injured by trauma or bad experiences: the defiant Solange Boshe, the idiot Harold Orley, and the violent Vsevolod Roznine. Generally, however, the inhabitants of the East American Parapsychological Research and Training Center are bright, gentle, honest, heroic people—a kind of collective superprotagonist. The founder of the center, Henry Darrow, is a man of principle whose foresight is broader than mere psychic precognition. His handling of the wager by which the Talented obtain Beechwoods, the Center site, in addition to his response to his fore-knowledge of his own and others' deaths, shows a man of superior wisdom. His last name, Darrow, suggesting Clarence Darrow (the man who defended the classroom teaching of evolution), emphasizes McCaffrey's theme of humankind's evolution. There is the suggestion that *To Ride Pegasus* is about the birth of a new race of humans, the Talented. Hence the emphasis on pregnancy; not just Ruth, but Pat Tawfik, is pregnant. The egg motif (see below) may be part of this imagery, also.

At times, McCaffrey suggests that Talent is latent in all humankind and that its absence is the result of brain injury (*TRP* 73). Mostly, however, she sees the Talented as one rung higher on the evolutionary ladder from animal to God. Just as her constant appeal to rationality is drawn from Pope's *An Essay on Man,* so is her imagery of the god-like qualities of the Talented. Hence Senator Mansfield Zeusman (the name suggests both *man* and *Zeus,* but he has thrown in with the side of *man's field*) chooses a passage from the First Epistle in *An Essay on Man* to make it seem that the Talented are "playing god": "Who sees with equal eye, as God of all,/A hero perish or a sparrow fall" (*TRP* 60; *An Essay on Man,* Epistle I, 11. 87–88). In this passage, Pope is explaining that, just as a lamb would not be happy if it could see that humans were planning its useful death, so humankind is not granted foreknowledge of its fate because God does not want people to be unhappy. The implication is that the Talented, especially those with precognition, are nearer to a god-like state because they *do* know their own times of death. Likewise, when op Owen suggests that the Talented reply to Zeusman, "Whatever is, is right" (*TRP* 62; *An Essay on Man,* Epistle I, 1. 294), he is comparing God's will in the human world to the result of Talented intervention—a sunny response to Andres's "What will be, will be," a negative, fatalistic sentiment from Christopher Marlowe's *Doctor Faustus* (1. 1. 48, slightly paraphrased). Finally, op Owen suggests that the Talented and their legislative advocates have the task to "Be candid where we can but vindicate the ways of God to man" (*TRP* 62; *An Essay on Man,* Epistle I, 11. 15–16). But it is the ways of the Talented that Andres must vindicate to the non-Talented. The suggestion is not, to be sure, that the Talented have actually attained godhood. Just as *An Essay on Man* emphasizes humanity's "middle state" (Epistle II, 1. 3), McCaffrey's Talented hang "between, in doubt to act or rest" (*TRP* 83; *An Essay on Man,* Epistle II, 1. 7). The Talented are still somewhere on Pope's chain of being, below God, but above non-Talented mankind. To emphasize the limitations even of the Talented, op Owen comments on Ruth Horvath's ability to control her child's genetic heritage; "One science only will one genius fit./So vast is art, so narrow human wit!" (*TRP* 120; *An Essay on Criticism,* 11. 60–61, punctuation adjusted by McCaffrey). Ruth may be a genius, but only in one very limited area. So with all the Talented—more god-like than the non-Talented, but not actually gods themselves.

Throughout *To Ride Pegasus,* psychic ability is compared to artistic ability, and the horse-and-rider metaphor is used to illuminate both types of human "flying." The image of the Talented being the rider of a winged horse, a pegasus, is developed at some length at least seven times in the book (*TRP* 11, 56, 163–164, 181, 195, 206, 243), not counting titles. Riding pegasus—i.e., practicing psychic abilities—is depicted as being thrilling by elevating the rider above the rest of humankind, dangerous, a way of getting a superior view, and a sign of courage. However, the winged horse requires a bridle (human control) to avoid getting singed by the sun (unrestrained, self-indulgent emotion). In several of the pegasus images, the idea of poetic inspiration is specifically invoked. Pegasus is a "poetic winged horse of flights of fancy" (*TRP* 11) and particularly "the symbol of poetry . . . flights of verbal fantasy" (*TRP* 163–164). McCaffrey is equating the artistic gift with the psychic gift and representing both with the pegasus, or horse-and-rider, image. Hence, Dorotea's telepathic gift "might as well be drawing freehand" (*TRP* 87). The very use of Pope's *An Essay on Man* and *An Essay on Criticism*—in addition to quotations from Marlowe (*TRP* 62), Spenser (*TRP* 36), Butler (*TRP* 135), Kipling (*TRP* 165), and Shakespeare (*TRP* 232)—suggest that McCaffrey's theme is not just psychic Talent, but also artistic talent, that is, imagination. Finally, one of the leading characters, Amalda, is in fact a performing artist who has portrayed Charmian in Shakespeare's *Antony and Cleopatra* and later becomes a folksinger. Amalda is one of McCaffrey's "singing heroines," like Helva, Killashandra, and Menolly. A comparison between Talent and art is thus implied; both faculties are depicted as riding a winged horse. Here is another appearance of the horse-and-rider motif.

To emphasize the flight symbol in another way, McCaffrey uses extensive bird imagery. Amalda is represented as a "flitting bird" (*TRP* 185, 187, 201, 236); the center's lawyers are "legal eagles" (*TRP* 209); Welch swears "by God's little chickens" (*TRP* 210); the street down which Solange Boshe runs to escape is "Oriole" (*TRP* 146); Welch, having found Amalda's hideout, like a cat, is "covered with canary feathers" (*TRP* 189). Even the Pope quotation on precognition involves the fall of a "hero or a *sparrow*" (*TRP* 60). Birds have eggs; McCaffrey uses eggs in the dragon books and in *Dinosaur Planet* to suggest both birth and flight. In *To Ride Pegasus,* op Owen reflects that you can't "make an omelette without breaking eggs" (*TRP* 222) and regards Amaldo and Roznine as "two baskets with the same eggs" (*TRP* 232). Even the machine that detects Talent is nicknamed the Goosegg!

The world of *To Ride Pegasus* is not as fully developed as other McCaffrey worlds, and it is not the tour de force that *Dragonflight* is. Because some of the chapters appeared first as shorter pieces, the philosophical implications of Talent and the horse-and-rider motif are somewhat obscured in response to editorial necessities. So it is with the depiction of Ruth Horvath, who seems a bit weak for a liberated woman. Her lack of confidence in her own maternal ability, in addition to op Owen's decision not to tell her what her psychic gift is, for example, may seem to some readers a bit condescending. But *To Ride Pegasus* is an important book in McCaffrey's canon because it reveals her philosophical attitude toward human evolution and elaborates on the pegasus image, developing the motif of horse and rider.

The stories in *Get Off the Unicorn* span a period in McCaffrey's publishing history from 1959 to 1977. Since the theme of psychic ability recurs in several of them, it is illuminating to consider them with *To Ride Pegasus*. In fact, "Apple" is reprinted in *Get Off the Unicorn*. And the titles of both books refer to riding fabulous beasts, though McCaffrey explains in her Introduction that the working title of the later book was *Get of the Unicorn:* a reference to beings *begotten* by unicorns. A typographical error resulted in the published title of the book, which thus by chance suggests a rider dismounting from a unicorn—another instance of the horse-and-rider motif.

In addition to the stories themselves, *Get Off the Unicorn* contains insightful comments by McCaffrey on her own fiction. Her grouping of the stories also suggests thematic relationships. Here she also uses the short-story format to experiment with first-person narration ("Horse from a Different Sea"), unreliable narrator ("Great Canine Chorus"), naive narrator ("A Proper Santa Claus"), the mystery story ("Weather on Welladay"), and erotica ("The Thorns of Barevi").

"Lady in the Tower" and "A Meeting of Minds" are far-future stories, which might, McCaffrey says, someday be part of a novel called *The Bitter Tower*. "Lady in the Tower" is the story McCaffrey prefers to acknowledge as her first published story, though "Freedom of the Race" predates it by six years. The premise of the two Bitter Tower stories is that the abilities described in *To Ride Pegasus* have evolved into much more powerful talents. "Lady in the Tower" is a love story about Rowan, a woman so gifted that she cannot find a lover in spite of her beauty and spirit because she is unable to relate to a man who lacks her telepathic and telekinetic gift and few men are equal to her in talent. She finally "meets" a charming telepath equal to her in ability, but he lives light-years away, near the star Deneb. They can communicate only mentally because she is inhibited from teleporting herself across space, a curse of the talented in her world. But this charismatic lover, Jeff Raven, discovers how to break this inhibition, and the two are able to teleport and consummate their love.

McCaffrey loves to reverse plots, so the second story, "A Meeting of Minds," turns the premise of the first story upside down. Years later, Rowan's daughter Damia also finds herself isolated by her psychic gifts. She too meets a lover telepathically, but the lover is a psychically gifted alien. Damia feels this is no barrier to their love; perhaps he is humanoid. However, it turns out that he is a kamikaze brain-ship sent by aliens to destroy her civilization. She does get a lover at the end of the story, but he is an old family friend, the green-skinned, physically handsome Afra, who has joined in battle with her against the alien when the latter's treachery has become apparent.

Though there is no implication that the Bitter Tower stories are part of the same series as *To Ride Pegasus*, McCaffrey uses the same theoretical framework and the same vocabulary for both worlds. Psychic gifts are described as *talent* in both. Imagery of birds expands the flying motif in the Bitter Tower stories as it did in *To Ride Pegasus*. The talented are "golden geese" (*GOTU* 3); Jeff Raven is a "cocky young rooster" (*GOTU* 19); the alien Sodan is "winging" his way toward Damia (*GOTU* 36); the eldest talent lives near the star Altair, which is in Aquila, or the Eagle. Rowan's name is that of a tree, a stationary launching platform for birds; when she marries Jeff Raven, she too becomes a "raven"—a bird—as do her children. Through him, she is granted flight.

McCaffrey's early work almost always has fairy-tale imagery, too; Rowan is like Rapunzel, locked in a tower by old man Jupiter, just as Callisto (the Jovian moon she inhabits) is the name of one of Jupiter's lovers imprisoned in the sky with her son as Ursa Major and Ursa Minor. Damia's fairy tale is Cinderella, only her "Prince Charming" (*GOTU* 56) proves more deadly than charming.

There are three other stories about psychic gifts in *Get Off the Unicorn*, all of which depict a present-day world before Daffyd op Owen and the Parapsychological Center. Specifically, they depict children with psychic gifts, showing how present-day society inhibits these gifts. "Great Canine Chorus," "Finder's Keeper," and "A Proper Santa Claus" all exhibit McCaffrey's unerring touch in the portrayal of children.

"The Great Canine Chorus" is about a relationship between a German shepherd, Wizard, who actually was owned by McCaffrey, and a physically handicapped girl who communicates telepathically with him, though she refuses to speak to his policeman companion. Though the characterization is somewhat like that of Solange Boshe, the world-set is not exactly that of *To Ride Pegasus,* because the girl, Maria Barres, has several psychic abilities and the Talented in *To Ride Pegasus* have only one each. Maria is a victim of poverty who is discovered by a small-time numbers runner. The pair soon learn that she can extend her talents to filching drugs telekinetically. However, when she telepathically calls all the dogs in Wilmington, Delaware, to help defend her during a minor acccident, she is trampled and apparently killed. Only the last sentence in the story suggests that she is not dead but has transferred her consciousness elsewhere and still communicates with Wizard. McCaffrey uses the first person in this sentence only, one of her few examples of narrative trickery *or* first-person narrative.

Maria is clearly the victim of adult manipulation. Too young to judge how best to use her talent, she allows herself to be used by petty criminals who destroy her. McCaffrey gets the reader to see the world from Maria's point of view: she wants good food, pretty clothes, and the music of bird's song. Nothing in her background has suggested that she should trust hospitals or police officers. The dog Wizard (a charming touch is achieved when she tricks the dog's companion into giving him a banana) is nearer to her size, so she trusts him.

The flight image occurs in this story as it has in *To Ride Pegasus* and the Bitter Towers stories: Maria is fond of birds and gets her adult exploiters to buy her a whole cage of canaries. The petty criminal himself is Jack *Finch*, and a finch is a kind of songbird.

"Finder's Keeper" is also about a child with psychic ability—this time the ability to find lost objects. The child, Peter Kiernan, manages to conceal his talent from his rich acquaintance Mr. Roche (who reminds one of a *roach,* perhaps) but is found out by his mother's greasy boyfriend, Ken Fargo (who thinks that he and Peter will *go far* together). Fargo is an insurance investigator and wants to use Peter to get insurance rewards—plus the love of Peter's mother. Peter distrusts Fargo and convinces him that a concussion has destroyed his psychic talent. There is a hint that the physician who attends Peter, Dr. Wingard (who *guards* this young *winner*), is telepathic because he immediately assures Fargo that Peter is very ill and will be a financial burden rather than a source of income. Peter is the only child in this group whose story ends rather happily; he looks forward to using his gift as an adult without being victimized by those more powerful than he.

"A Proper Santa Claus," the story of a six-year-old with the gift of animating his childish drawings and making them real or "proper," is a quiet masterpiece. McCaffrey's ability to identify in a totally unsentimental way with a child's point of view, together with her vision of childish artistic talent destroyed by adult clichés, creates an emotional impact out of proportion with the length of this unpretentious but powerful short story.

The story is told from the viewpoint of the little boy, Jeremy North, so the immensity of his psychic gift only slowly dawns on the reader. The opening of the story seems quite conventional—until Jeremy picks up and eats a cookie he has just painted. Later in the story, he attempts to give his father a "proper" car he has painted—presumably one that could actually be driven—but the father kindly refuses to witness the transformation of the car from paint into reality; though Jeremy is a "Picasso," the father gives the painting back. Jeremy finally loses faith in adult ability to understand or witness his gift and begins to conceal such creations as water-soluble Hallowe'en monsters. At Christmas, however, he creates a "proper" Santa Claus, one that is going to bring Jeremy all the presents he wants. His teacher discovers him dressing the tiny, naked Santa and brightly lectures him on "the spirit of giving and sharing, of good fellowship" (*GOTU* 215). Jeremy is horrified to realize that he has been so selfish and resolves never to make anything "proper" again.

The power of the story resides in its portrayal of childlike imagination—"primitive magic" (*GOTU* 215) against the unimaginative sentimentality of adults. It is also a parable of art: Jeremy possesses an artistic gift unsullied by adult clichés and cynicism. Though his parents and teacher are kind, they do not have the power of belief that Jeremy needs to make his creation "proper." They ultimately destroy this belief in him. So with the artist: art, like Jeremy's Santa Claus project, is utterly selfish and goal-directed. The minute it becomes contaminated by the socially acceptable goals society imposes on the artist, the artistic gift loses its power. Though McCaffrey may endorse socially useful or didactic art elsewhere, the highest art, as with Menolly's "joy in music" (*Dsinger* 122), is totally free of mundane concerns and interpretational clichés.

The horse-and-rider metaphor appears several times and in several guises in this marvelous story. The car Jeremy paints for his father is a substitute for a horse—a mechanical, inanimate substitute because of the father's lack of imagination. The father, after all, prefers an Andy Warhol soup can to a Picasso. The Green Horse with pink mane and tail that gallops around Jeremy's room is an emblem of the evanescent quality of artistic inspiration. It brushes against a wall and, since Jeremy created it of chalk pastels, it is erased. The reindeer of dull plasticene with their jerry-rigged harnesses are intended to carry Jeremy's artistic creation on its intended flight. Their fate—to be gilded in response to the criticism of little Cynthia, and ultimately to be abandoned as not in conformity with the "true" (i.e., adult) spirit of Christmas—represents the ultimate defeat of Jeremy's artistic gift. Neither he, nor they, will ever fly.

"A Proper Santa Claus" was edited toward a more up-beat ending for Roger Elwood's *Demon Kind*,[4] but McCaffrey fortunately restored her original ending in *Get Off the Unicorn*. The story, as McCaffrey intended it, is a sad and perfect jewel.

"Daughter" and "Dull Drums" are stories about Nora Fenn, an insecure but intelligent girl whose self-confidence has been somewhat damaged by her close-minded father, who, in their future world, had "ordered" two sons but got a son and a daughter. The first story shows that Nora can turn her father's partiality toward her brother to advantage because it makes her work all the harder for paternal approval, while the second shows that Nora can liberate herself from the stinginess and rigidity of her father and at the same time triumph over the manipulative males in her ill-chosen major. Both are, in a sense, stories of feminine liberation and the battle between the sexes. The relationship between Nora's mother and father is a particular point of interest, as is Nora's relationship with the young man who defends her against her father's tyranny and her fellow students' exploitiveness. At the end of the second story, Nora begins to think for herself at long last, evidence that she has thrown off the shackles of family sexism.

The ideas in the Nora Fenn stories relate to a number of other McCaffrey tales. Nora is victimized, as Sara Fulton is in *Restoree*, by her own family. The Cinderella motif also is evident in the Nora Fenn stories, as it is in *Dragonsinger*, for example. The Fenn in "Cinderella Switch" (in Judy-Lynn del Rey's *Stellar #6*, New York: Ballantine, 1980, pp. 110–121) is not Nora's brother, but perhaps some descendant, suggesting that George Fenn could not keep his descendants down on the farm, in spite of his egocentric bossiness.

"Changeling," "The Thorns of Barevi," and "A Horse from a Different Sea" belong to a genre that could be called future-sex stories. They all concern ways in which sex and reproduction could be different than they are in our here-and-now world. "Changeling" is about a highly unconventional family arrangement in a future-world where the nuclear family has changed to the extent that the thought of having a kitchen—a room devoted only to food preparation—is ludicrous to an architect. Claire Simonsen, the heroine, finds herself the "wife" of three men: one homosexual, one bisexual, and one heterosexual who is her legal husband. The incident of the story is her delivering the homosexual's son in a remote retreat where he has taken her to enjoy the exultation of having his own son, against all social customs. There is a hint that each of the four "partners" loves one of the others unrequitedly: Claire's heterosexual legal husband loves her, while Claire loves the homosexual father of her child, etc. The treatment of unusual sexual preferences is challenging; fiction does not offer many such sympathetic portrayals of male homosexuality, although McCaffrey's *Moreta, Dragonlady of Pern* contains another such portrait.

"The Thorns of Barevi" is a tale of sex between a human woman and an alien male. Like the heroine of *Restoree*, Christin Bjornsen is kidnapped by aliens—in this case the cat-like Catteni. After a few months of slavery, she escapes and lives in the wilderness of a Catteni-dominated planet. Again as in *Restoree*, she rescues one of the alien males and is rewarded by his aggressive but pleasant sexual attentions. The title represents a metaphor: the thorn bushes discharge their missiles and rearm quickly; Catteni males likewise have a short recovery period after making love. "The Thorns of Barevi" is a diverting whimsy, hardly a serious piece of fiction. McCaffrey wrote the story as an experiment in soft-core pornography but became interested in nonerotic aspects of the Catteni, about whom she may one day write a whole novel.

"Horse from a Different Sea" is again about human/alien sex, but this time human males are mated with alien females posing as prostitutes. The result, curiously, is that, as with sea horses, the human males become pregnant. The story is unusual in that it is written in the first person, with a hard-bitten, cynical, general practitioner as narrator. The use of colloquial language is very successful in producing the seedy characterizations. Interestingly, McCaffrey once more introduces her horse-and-rider image. One of the pregnant males is Explorer Scout Horace Baker (*GOTU* 169). His name contains many puns. *Horace* sounds a bit like *horse*; the narrator compares the male pregnancy with that of a sea *horse* (hence the title). Also, previously, pregnancy has been referred to as "buns in the oven" (*GOTU* 168), so it's appropriate that a pregnant person is a "Baker." Though the story seems to have little to do with art (which is a tenor in the horse-and-rider metaphor), *Horace* is, after all, the name of a Latin poet. The doctor's attitude toward the male pregnancies seems to be more awe and wonder than horror (as in the comparable Jack Finney's *The Invasion of the Body Snatchers*), and the alien suicides in a blaze of light in a brothel run by Linda (the name means *light*). Perhaps the pregnancies are a bit like an epidemic of imagination.

"Weather on Welladay" is a mystery story, written at the request of Judy-Lynn del Rey to match a cover for *Galaxy*. What McCaffrey came up with was a world of radioactive-iodine-bearing whales. The mystery is who is pirating the thyroid product, thus creating a critical shortage of the iodine and endangering the whales. It's a complicated and suspenseful yarn that McCaffrey says "stands alone" (*GOTU* 117), but apparently she liked Welladay and its whales enough to mention them in the *Continuum* version of the Killashandra story ("K—CS" 151) because Killashandra's love, Shad Tucker, has fished for Welladay whales.

Get Off the Unicorn also includes "The Smallest Dragonboy," another story exemplifying McCaffrey's sympathetic and original treatment of the child's point of view. This story, the hero of which has a name similar to McCaffrey's brother, is not part of any of the full-length dragon novels. It tells of a little boy, Keevan, who is thought to be too small to compete for the love of his very own dragon and whose hopes are smashed when an older bully injures him. However, he drags himself to the Hatching ground and Impresses Heth, a bronze dragon who inquires solicitously, *"Don't you like me?"* (*GOTU* 231), one of the most loaded questions in all McCaffrey's works. K'van appears as an adult rider of the bronze Heth in *The White Dragon* (*WD* 321). The story taps the same wellsprings of wonder as do all of McCaffrey's Flying, Hatching, and Impression scenes.

"Honeymoon" is a further development of the story of Helva and Niall Parollan, discussed in my chapter on *The Ship Who Sang*. "Apple" is discussed above, with *To Ride Pegasus*, although it stands alone very well.

These two books, a novel and a collection of shorter works, seem appropriate for discussion together because of similarities in theme and symbol. In both *To Ride Pegasus* and *Get Off the Unicorn*, exercise of the imaginative gift is emblemized by the riding of a fabulous horse-like creature and by an image of flight. Though these images are found throughout McCaffrey's works, they are most explicit in these two works, and the horse-and-rider motif receives its most literal interpretation. This development of imagery in connection with imagination, talent, art, and the fabulous is of further interest because of the variety of stylistic treatments McCaffrey offers in the two volumes. Thoughtful examination of *To Ride Pegasus* and *Get Off the Unicorn* can illuminate *The Ship Who Sang,* the dragon books, and much of McCaffrey's other fiction.

NOTES

[1] "Absorbing the Miraculous," *New Worlds #6*, ed. Hilary Bailey and Charles Platt (New York: Avon, 1975), pp. 221-225. The British first edition of this is *New Worlds #7*, ed. Hilary Bailey and Charles Platt (London: Sphere, 1974).

[2] Sam J. Lundwall, *Science Fiction: What It's All About* (New York: Ace, 1971), pp. 154, 165.

[3] Susan Wood, "Women and Science Fiction," *Algol/Starship,* 16, No. 1, Whole Number 33 (Winter 1978-79), 11. Also see McCaffrey's own analysis of the story, "Hitch Your Dragon to a Star: Romance and Glamour in Science Fiction," in *Science Fiction, Today and Tomorrow,* ed. Reginald Bretnor (New York: Harper & Row, 1974), 282-283.

[4] (New York: Avon, 1973), pp. 100-109.

VI
KILLASHANDRA OF BALLYBRAN

Ballybran is atypical of McCaffrey's worlds. It is a cold world, where Killashandra Ree invokes privacy with a capital P, a world where men and women discard their reproductive potential on the promise of riches and extended life span, a world without marriage, without children, where sexuality is a bait to recruit further victims into the Guild, where loyalty is impossible because memory is unreliable.

There are two versions of Killashandra's story; the first was done as a series for Roger Elwood's *Continuum*. This one is composed of "Prelude to a Crystal Song," "Milekey Mountain," "Killashandra—Crystal Singer," and "Killashandra—Coda and Finale." Most McCaffrey aficionados are aware by now that "Killashandra—Crystal Singer" was published before "Milekey Mountain," in spite of the fact that "Milekey Mountain" takes place earlier. Each of the stories stands independently, but together they span Killashandra's life and include her death scene. The first two stories are adapted as episodes in *The Crystal Singer*.[1] *The Crystal Singer* is a more optimistic work, ending with Killashandra's triumphal return to the Ballybran system after mounting the crystal she has cut to create a communications system for a mining civilization. There are some inconsistencies between the *Continuum* stories and the novel version, which mainly reveal that McCaffrey developed the notion of the symbiotic spore of Ballybran after the *Continuum* stories were complete.

This chapter will explore the isolated coldness of McCaffrey's vision and show how this inorganic quality is supported through imagery and irony. Though the *Continuum* stories and *The Crystal Singer* are not part of a larger whole, contradicting each other as they do, their emotive vision and supporting imagery are mutually consistent.

The Crystal Singer confutes critics who claim McCaffrey has a single model of human love, nurturance, and family life, as we can demonstrate by contrasting Ballybran and Pern. People on Pern are generally monogamous and take joy in having children, while people on Ballybran have a reputation for being always alone (*CS* 56) and accept sterility as part of their adaptation to the planet. People on Pern live communally and seldom see money, while crystal singers are constantly aware of their net worth; their training in the Guild is a debt they must eventually work off. Robinton, a Guild Master of Pern, has a reputation of kindness and geniality. His relationship with his star pupil, Menolly, is kept on the highest plane. Lanzecki, a Guild Master of Ballybran, laughs only rarely and sexually exploits his star pupil, Killashandra, so that even she is reminded of the relationship of Svengali and Trilby (*CS* 190–191). The Pernese dragonriders have a symbiotic relationship with their dragons that comes to represent the imaginative soaring of the human heart in love and art. The corresponding symbiote in *The Crystal Singer* is colder and almost macabre.

Here is the horse-and-rider metaphor finally perverted almost to the unrecognizable. Again, we have the normal human linked with something that makes him or her above the rest of humankind, alien or superhuman. The Ballybran spore makes the crystal singer, like a vampire, long-lived (though not immortal) and grants heightening of senses. Again, ecstasy comes through the linkage—through the spore's affinity for crystal, which has a hard, cold beauty and value. The artistic metaphor is specifically invoked, in that perfect pitch is required to sing crystal. The name of the man who lures Killashandra into the Heptite Guild, *Carrik*, could echo the name of a famous British actor, David Garrick. The ecstatic trance the singer enters when handling crystal resembles the artistic enchantment of the engaged artist. Killashandra uses the language of operatic performance in connection with her craft: for example, her mounting of the black crystal for the Trundomoui is deliberately made as theatrical as possible, and her relationship with Fergil is referred to as a "duet" ("K–CF" passim). Crystal itself, like jade, "sings" or resonates when tapped.

But this metaphor for artistic experience emphasizes negative characteristics. For one thing, art is seen as addictive. Once a person has started singing crystal, she can never stop—Lanzecki being an exception. The planet itself lures the singers back; they begin to experience severe spinal pain after extended absence. Yet the singing itself is painful after awhile. To complicate matters, the singers often become so entranced with cutting crystal that they ignore physical danger and are killed by storms. Interestingly, the storms kill by crescendos of sound, sound that is particularly damaging to those attuned to crystal.

Like actors who "forget" their hometown buddies when they reach the top, crystal singers also forget—but they forget everything, including their chronological ages and their most recent lovers. To compensate, according to Lanzecki, photographic memory is a requisite for singing crystal (*CS* 186), just as it is helpful in acting. The loss of memory is an isolating factor; lack of memory means lack of gratitude (*CS* 238) and ultimately lack of human ties. Crystal itself isolates the crystal singer because of its beauty, value, and other properties—so with art. Killashandra, had she gone on to be an operatic star, would still have been isolated by her art. Singing crystal is a metaphor for art at its worst.

Coldness and impersonality are held as positive values on Ballybran. On the Rag Blue Swan Delta, Killashandra sees crystal singers as "proud, aloof, curiously radiant. . . . people apart" (*CS* 172). Conceit in a singer, says Lanzecki, is a virtue (*CS* 184). Rimbol, an engaging trainee who loves people, is "going to have to learn not to care so much about people now" (*CS* 172). Killashandra, returning from her first cutting trip, is "terrifying" (*CS* 221). Killashandra's relationships with men are similarly cold and impersonal. Shortly after she has spent her first night with Lanzecki, they greet each other with terse businesslike comments and part without a kiss or affectionate comment (*CS* 247). Her relationship with Carrik, before she goes to Ballybran, is more tender; she nurses him back to the Guild, feeling obliged because he rescued her from the depression of losing her operatic career. On Armagh III (in "Killashandra—Crystal Singer") she treats men as friends and sexual objects but is touched only by Shad— whom she leaves because she is too kind to make him a crystal singer. Others—Rimbol, for one—are friends, but not permanent partners. Finally, in "Killashandra—Coda and Finale," she is preyed upon sexually by Fergil, who pretends to be a former lover so that he can take over her claim after he has left her to die in a mach storm. And she is never sure that Lanzecki has not collaborated in Fergil's betrayal.

Just as romantic relationships lack warmth on Ballybran, so does the family. Since the crystal singers have willingly been infected with spore that makes them sterile, none of them have children. There is a reference in "Killashandra—Crystal Singer" to children Killashandra has had decades previous, but the beginning of *The Crystal Singer,* where young Killashandra has left her family to study for ten years with Valdi, makes no mention of her children. At any rate, Killashandra has no contact with whatever children she has or imagines she has had. Her own family has been unsympathetic to her music (*CS* 11). She senses her isolation from people like Shad Tucker to whom she is "not the sort of woman he'd build a home for on his acres of sea front" ("K—CS" 178–179).

Privacy is such a value on Killashandra's home world of Fuerte that in the British edition of *The Crystal Singer* the word is capitalized several times (*CS* 56, 60, 67). It is a word that appears frequently in the text and is apparently a concept carefully protected by law.

The coldness of interpersonal relations on Ballybran is reflected by the imagery of the book in many ways; numbers, geometric figures, and colors take the place of more organic imagery. The phrase "crystal in the blood" seems to echo the phrase "gold in the blood" from *The Treasure of the Sierra Madre,* sounding the impingement of the inorganic world on the organic. Valdi's furious epithet to Carrik, "silicate spider . . . crystal cuckoo" (*CS* 33), further emphasizes the invasion of the warm, human organism by something inorganic. Indeed, Killashandra has become part alien by the end of *The Crystal Singer,* when a nameless official suggests intimidating the crowd by carrying her through it. After all, he observes, "She's not a woman. She's a crystal singer!" (*CS* 292).

The sinister tonality of the book is reinforced with imagery, and particularly imagery from George DuMaurier's *Trilby,* of fishing, reversal of relationships, and a Black Mass.

Killashandra herself, in an instant of clarity (momentarily free of the delusions and tricks of the Heptite Guild), is "reminded of . . . a man who had hypnotized a girl, a musical idiot, into vocal performances without peer. . . . Ah . . . Zvengali" (*CS* 190–191). Indeed, there are similarities in characterization and in plot. The name *Lanzecki* is very nearly an anagram of *Zvengali* (as Killashandra remembers it). Lanzecki has retired from crystal singing, just as Svengali did not himself sing. Lanzecki uses almost hypnotic persuasion on Killashandra. Killashandra is a beautiful, headstrong girl, like Trilby, who is easily led into a trap by one who befriends her in a moment of crisis. That crystal singing is indeed a trap is apparent in occasional remarks, such as when Killashandra has stepped through the portal to join the Guild, "Then it was too late" (*CS* 79). Trilby and Killashandra are both singers, both with a major flaw in their talents. In Trilby's case, it is that she has a wondrous voice but is tone-deaf; in Killashandra's, it is the opposite: she has perfect pitch and wonderful training but has an unpleasant flaw in her voice. After Svengali's death, Trilby forgets her life with him (lived as it has been under hypnosis). Killashandra, too, develops memory problems after she begins her career of singing cyrstal.

One of the richest parallels between *Trilby* and *The Crystal Singer* involves the spider image. Crystal singers are referred to again and again as "crystal cuckoos, silicate spiders" (*CS* 33, 81, 156). Killashandra sees herself upon her return from her first crystal song as a "Warp Widow" (*CS* 228). Clearly, McCaffrey intends to emphasize the spider image. Chances are strong that McCaffrey's childhood copy of *Trilby* was one of the very common early editions on the cover of which, embossed in gold, is a winged heart trapped in a spider's web and menaced by a spider. Even had McCaffrey not seen this cover, DuMaurier frequently likens Svengali to a spider.

The "silicate spider, crystal cuckoo" image is a sinister and complex one that goes beyond literary references. Cuckoos, traditionally, lay their eggs in other birds' nests and thus allow their young to be raised at the expense of the other birds' families. The Ballybran spore is similarly parasitic, reproducing itself at the expense of the hosts' reproductive powers. Spiders, ironically, are *victims* of a similar predatory reproductive cycle; spider wasps paralyze spiders and lay eggs within their bodies. McCaffrey may have had this parallel in mind when characterizing the crystal-singing carriers of Ballybran spore. She refers to the spore as a symbiote, but it is only slightly more beneficient than cuckoos and spider wasps. The crystal singers are indeed half-alien, hosts to a parasite that gives and takes away at the same time.

Trilby's surname, O'Farrell, is Irish, and McCaffrey emphasizes the Irish in her depiction of Ballybran and other worlds in the crystal singer universe. Ballybran's moon, Shankill, has a real Irish place name, meaning *old church*. Another place-name on Ballybran, Balinteer (*CS* 136), means *carpenter's town*.[2] *Shilmore, Shanganagh*, and *Ballybran* are apparently coinages made from real morphemes of Irish place-name etymology. *Ballybran*, for example, seems to be from *Bally, town* or *homestead;* and *bran, raven*—an appropriately sinister name.

Irish flavoring also permeates "Killashandra—Crystal Singer" in *Continuum II*. The planet, *Armagh*, is named after a county in Northern Ireland. *Trefoil*, the name of the city, means *three-leaf*, a reference to shamrocks. There is a reference to Parnell's world, possibly after Charles

Stewart Parnell, the Irish nationalist hero. There are also some Irish-sounding names, such as Shamus Thursday and the Murtagh River.

However, Irish etymologies in the book and in the *Continuum* story do more than refer to Trilby's Irishness. The first crystal singer that Killashandra ever meets is named Carrik. The crystal singer who, in "Killashandra—Coda and Finale," lures her to her death, is named Fergil. These two names appear to be parts of the name of an Irish seaport, Carrickfergus, meaning Fergus's Rock, after the Irish folk hero. Thus Killashandra goes from the *rock* (crystal) to the wielder of a magic sword (really a sonic cutter), *Fergus* (Fergil), who finally vanquishes her. Thus the two names suggest a fatal closed cycle—Carrik at the beginning, Fergil at the end.

But there is still another function for these touches of Irish flavor. They also evoke a fishing image, another suggestion that the new crystal singers are caught by a bait or a trap.

Killashandra wonders idly why her fellow recruits are referred to as "much of a catch?" (*CS* 81, 141). None of them has become suspicious at the repeated disclaimers that all must sign assuring that the Guild did not coerce them to join; none wonders at the fact that most have been abruptly frustrated in the pursuit of a brilliant career. Yet they are like fish; when Killashandra goes to Armagh, in "Killashandra—Crystal Singer," Lanzecki urges her to find a new partner and bring him back to sing crystal with her ("K—CS" 139). So she goes to a fishing town on a sea-world, and the lover she eventually selects is a fisherman called Shad—and *shad* is also a variety of fish commonly used as food.

The man who welcomes Killashandra to her quarters on Shankill is called Ford, and Shankill is the portal to Ballybran, almost like a body of water, a ford, one must cross to reach one's destination. Killashandra, like all crystal singers, is fond of seafood (*CS* 16, 54) and of water-worlds ("K—CS" 159). And the man who provides her sonic cutter is nameless except for the epithet, the Fisherman (*CS* 160).

While the above types of imagery persist throughout the *Continuum* stories and *The Crystal Singer*, each version has a pattern that provides its own unity. The *Continuum* series is based on a series of love relationships and reversals, and *The Crystal Singer* is patterned after a Black Mass.

The parallelism of the *Continuum* stories is pointed up by the way each ends—the first three with an invocation to memory, the last with the end of all memory, in Killashandra's death. The cycle begins and ends with Killashandra as victim, and the two middle stories show her refusing to victimize someone else as she is victimized. "Prelude to a Crystal Song" is paired with "Killashandra—Crystal Singer," and "Milekey Mountain" is paired with "Killashandra—Coda and Finale."

What most reviewers seem to miss about the beginning of the Killashandra story is that the story is told by a naive narrator. Any reasonable attempt to guess Carrik's motivation in "Prelude to a Crystal Song" makes it clear that he has come to Fuerte hoping to find a partner. His exclamation, "What fantastic luck! . . . unbelievable luck . . . Fate, destiny, Karma, Lequol, Fidalkoram" ("PCS" 138), strikes us as almost raving. Yes, it is coincidence. Carrik probably thought he'd have to go father than the spaceport to find his prey. At one point he does tell Killashandra that she doesn't want to be a crystal singer, but his evasive tactics only inflame her curiosity, as they are probably meant to. Even if he vacillates, he does agree to let her join the Guild—as long as she tells him it's by her own free consent. But Killashandra, in her bullheaded naivete, is missing lots of cues —especially the fact that the very term *crystal singer* is considered a euphemism ("PCS" 142, *CS* 23), and euphemisms by definition are nice words for something bad—like "lady of the night" for *prostitute*. Indeed, there is strong evidence that Killashandra did *not* have a flawed voice at all—that Valdi was brought off by the powerful, wealthy Guild. After all, she had been the best singer in her class—how could she suddenly have developed a vocal flaw? Valdi's melodramatic scene at the spaceport, when he confronts Carrik and attempts to prevent Killashandra from becoming a crystal singer, could be sincere. Perhaps Valdi did not realize that the Guild had such malevolent intentions toward his prize student. Or perhaps Valdi's angry words are mere empty histrionics. In any case, Killashandra seems the helpless, innocent victim of sinister forces the reader sees dimly, but Killashandra sees not at all.

"Killashandra—Crystal Singer" exactly parallels the action of "Prelude to a Crystal Song," except that the roles are reversed. Killashandra, advised by Lanzecki to find a new crystal-singing partner off-world, goes to Armagh III, a fishing world. There she encounters her "fish," Shad Tucker. Like Carrik, she is delighted that her new friend has perfect pitch. As Carrik encounters Killashandra at a moment of crisis and defeat, Killashandra encounters Shad at the inverse, a moment of victory: the end of a successful *lunk*-hunting season. As Carrik has done with her, she impresses her young, innocent partner with physical beauty and sexual abandon; she also, like Carrik, evades his questions about her profession. As Carrik did with her, she celebrates the new passion with aquatic sports and fish dinners. Like Carrik, she is warned that she must return, when spinal pain wracks her after lovemaking. But—reversing the outcome of Carrik's dalliance with her—she chooses *not* to tell Shad she's a crystal singer and therefore she does not recruit him. Carrik is destroyed by an accident on his off-world vacation; Killashandra survives. Both, however, are still partnerless.

To point up the parallels, Killashandra asks herself at the end of the story, "Had she been lured to Ballybran by some ageless lover? Perhaps. Who knew?" ("K—CS" 179–180).

The other two *Continuum* stories also show a pattern of parallelism and reversal. In "Milekey Mountain," Killashandra is paired with Ardlor (in *The Crystal Singer,* his name is changed to Moksoon), who is to initiate her to crystal singing. Lanzecki arranges the pairing, explaining that Killashandra must be shepherded on her first trip. Ardlor is so disoriented from the crystal singers' memory disease that Killashandra has to force him back into his flitter (sled, in *The Crystal Singer*) to save his life when a "mach storm" threatens. However, she is penalized for her act of mercy; the Guild has no provisions for singers who are softhearted enough to put human life above financial self-interest.

In "Killashandra—Coda and Finale," it is Killashandra who has assumed the role of the older, more disoriented singer. She is encouraged to escort a younger singer, Fergil (his name suggests Vergil, who escorts Dante to Hell). When a mach storm is imminent, Fergil does *not* rescue Killashandra but leaves her maniacally carving a crystal tomb in the heart of her claim—the location of which Fergil has tricked out of her.

In both cases, Lanzecki sanctions the pairing. After it is too late, Killashandra even wonders if he conspired with Fergil so that the younger singer might obtain her claim—in the novel version, Killashandra has taken over a dead, older singer's claim. In both *Continuum* stories, Lanzecki cautions the younger singer not to let the older one turn off the storm alarms. In both stories, the younger singer becomes entranced by the first crystal cut; the implication is that Fergil may very well be cutting his very first crystal, unbeknownst to Killashandra. Even the name of Killashandra's rejected partner in "Coda and Finale," *Larsdahl,* is nearly an anagram of *Ardlor,* the name of the unwilling shepherd in "Milekey Mountain."

The role reversal, however, is turned upside down, just as it is in the other pair of stories, because Killashandra is kind and trusting. She never becomes so saturated with crystal (or whatever it is that makes crystal singers inhuman) that she can harm an innocent person or believe that another person can betray her. Carrik and Fergil victimize her; she doesn't suspect their treachery. She falters when the time comes to victimize Ardlor and Shad; she doesn't realize that treachery must become a way of life with a crystal singer.

Echoes of the reversal appear in the novel version; Killashandra is always looking in mirrors, and her name, *Killashandra,* reverses the syllables in the name of the moon that is Ballybran's link with the normal human world—*Shankill.* Ballybran itself is a world of reversal, where crystal ranges are deeps, not heights (*CS* 98).

The Roman Catholic Mass is a simultaneous reenactment of Christ's Last Supper and of the Crucifixion. A Black Mass, traditionally, is a parodic, blasphemous reenactment of the Mass. Typically, elements in the Christian Mass are inverted: the Lord's Prayer, for example, may be said backwards. Killashandra's mounting of crystal for the Trundamoux communications system resembles a Black Mass.

The tone of *The Crystal Singer,* we have already seen, reverberates with many diabolic elements. Some further examples would be the reference to one crystal singer, Fugastri, as "a devil." The sorter Enthor's eyes are red from his spore adaptation. Ballybran's dwellings, like its crystal ranges, are underground, and the more prestigious apartments are the deepest. All editions of *The Crystal Singer* contain thirteen chapters, evidence that McCaffrey rearranged chapters in the American edition to preserve the use of this diabolic number.

Killashandra is an appropriate celebrant for a Black Mass. Her name contains the rearranged syllables of the moon's name, *Shankill,* meaning *old church.* She is attuned to black crystal, and this tuning takes place when she unpacks a thirteen-piece set of black crystal. She is a woman, while the celebrant of the Christian Mass is a man; she robes herself in black. We have already spoken of fish imagery in connection with Killashandra and crystal singing; Christ suggested that his apostles become fishers of men. Demons can fish, too, apparently.

The actual mounting ceremony follows the general lines of a Black Mass. Like Christ's Last Supper (the first Christian Mass), it takes place at Passover. Passover on Ballybran is a time when the three moons pass over headquarters at once, a time of storm and upheaval like the earthquakes at Christ's death. The ceremony is an agonizing ordeal for Killashandra; it involves establishing a pentangle, or five-point figure, of black crystal, just as necromancy is often practiced within a pentangle. The black crystal itself—"Christ-al"—is a kind of blasphemous eucharist—alien, inorganic, dangerous, mysterious, an object of awe.

The mounting of the crystal complete, Killashandra echoes Christ's words, "I thirst" (John 19:28) (*CS* 292). Her inhumanity, the inverse of Christ's divinity, is affirmed: "She's not a woman. She's a crystal singer!" (*CS* 292). Like Christ on the cross, she is offered drink and, the ordeal over, carried away. As Christ lay in the tomb three days, Killashandra sleeps three days while the ordinary mortals around her assume that she's in a coma.

As elsewhere, McCaffrey's subtle ironies are overlooked by reviewers and critics. Amelia A. Rutledge finds that Killashandra's repeated successes at crystal singing suggest too little conflict.[3] But the conflict is more subtle, based as it is on the betrayal of a particularly talented victim—Killashandra. Rutledge also puzzles over the relationship with Lanzecki. Again, Lanzecki is more than a love interest; he is a complex, teasing element in the plot, since he probably seduces Killashandra because of her extraordinary talent and to maximize her usefulness to the Heptite Guild. Killashandra is a rare bird among science-fiction heroines—a naive observer to whom everything seems to be going just fine, even as the reader can see her being entangled more and more completely in the web of the "silicate spider." Such subtle irony is unusual in science fiction and therefore easy to overlook. But it is there.

McCaffrey's vision of the universe almost precludes pure evil. Misery in her world is usually the result of stupidity and lack of education. *The Crystal Singer,* with its macabre imagery and subtle undercurrents of betrayal, is therefore unique in her canon. As a result, Killashandra and Lanzecki are among her most fascinating human characters—Killashandra is a flawed, bitchy, but golden-hearted prima donna; Lanzecki the suave personification of seductive manipulation.

NOTES

[1] American editions omit the definite article. There are significant differences between the British first edition (see Bibliography) and American editions, including chapter renumbering and phraseology.

[2] See P.W. Joyce, *The Origin and History of Irish Names of Places,* 2nd ed. (Dublin: McGlashen & Gill, 1870). Again, this is a work that supplies "common wisdom" rather than scientific accuracy about etymologies—the sort of knowledge that McCaffrey uses symbolically.

[3] "McCaffrey, Anne. *The Crystal Singer*" (review), *Science Fiction & Fantasy Book Review,* issue 6, July/August 1982, pp. 29-30.

VII

THE DINOSAUR PLANET BOOKS, TWO NOVELLAS, UNCOLLECTED SHORT STORIES, THREE ROMANCES, AND MISCELLANEOUS WORK

The purpose of this chapter is to examine works of McCaffrey's that, by virtue of length or genre, do not lend themselves to individual chapters but that possess literary interest both because of their relationships to themes and motifs in other major works and because of their intrinsic merits. Of these, *Dinosaur Planet* and *Dinosaur Planet Survivors* show promise of requiring fuller analysis but only sketch in the outlines of a more ambitious saga. "The Greatest Love" and *The Coelura* are novella-length works (although *The Coelura* was published as a separate volume) that represent McCaffrey's recent thematic development. Six short stories demonstrate McCaffrey's skill in use of the shorter form. Three non-science-fiction novels (variously called romances, mysteries, or gothics) represent her work in the mainstream. A cookbook and an anthology of work by other writers require brief descriptions. Certain threads run through all these works: fairy-tale imagery, particularly of Cinderella; the triumph of imagination, as represented in the horse-and-rider motif; and feminism, as represented by the courageous, resourceful female protagonist.

Dinosaur Planet reads like the introduction to a much larger work. All elements seem to beg for much more extended treatment. The characters—members of an interstellar exploratory team looking for uranium and other energy sources on Ireta, a garlic-scented planet—seem too many and far too leisurely developed for such a short work. The point-of-view characters, Varian and Kai, seem at first bland and far too nice, which perhaps only reflects their upbringing in a civilization that has eliminated violence, ignorance, sexual possessiveness, and sexual discrimination. Attractive but gentle souls, they accept perfect equality with each other, along with a protective attitude toward the members of the team they co-lead. They are vegetarians and look with horror not just upon the ugly bloodlust of meat-eating teammates but upon the predatory activities of animals in their environment. There is no conflict between them except for gentle humor, and their sexual bond is discreet but totally lacking in the playful coyness of McCaffrey's lovers in other books. In fact, Kai's suggestion, "You know, it'd be nice if we practiced some sex ourselves" (*DP* 137) strikes the reader as rather chillingly direct.

Yet there are complexities suggested in the two: they are initiates in a practice called Discipline, an apparently yogic state that grants them strength and freedom from pain in emergency situations.

The other characters include three rather attractive, clever children; the boy proves brave enough to be the most interesting person in the story. Two of the scientists, Gaber and Trizein, have foibles enough to interest us. The heavy-worlders, whose bioengineered adaptation to high-gravity worlds somehow short-circuits their moral inhibitions in addition to making them carnivores, are interesting as a group but not individuated enough to be more than the villains of the piece. Two aliens are delightful innovations on McCaffrey's part: one, Vrl, comes from an avian race whose subjective time runs much faster than humans'. He is also amusingly paranoid. The other, Tor, belongs to a silicate-based race easily confused with rocks. Tor's subjective time runs much slower than humans', so that communication from him is often in the form of a single, very significant word.

Setting and plot (often closely related in science fiction) seem devoted to presenting one puzzle after another. Ireta—the planet's name means *angry*—appears to be in a state of evolution parallel to Earth's mezozoic period. However, cytological studies show that the flora and fauna of the planet seem to have arisen from widely different sources—in fact, from different planets. One totally alien animal, the "fringe," even has a hinged trapezoidal skeleton. Most puzzling, four exact duplicates of creatures from Earth's own prehistoric past are represented: tyrannosaurus rex, hadrosaurus, pteranodon, and hyracotherium. Even more puzzling, hyracotherium, the ancestor of the modern horse, could not be the wildest stretch of the imagination be contemporary with the other three. McCaffrey depicts the pterandon as an engaging, golden-furred avian with adorably curious young and advanced enough intelligence to weave nets to catch fish. Varian, before she becomes aware of their true identity, calls these "giffs."

Other pieces of the puzzle include the lengendary, evil "Others," who destroy life. Then, too, there is the fact the million-year-old beacons, or "cores," have already been put on the planet Ireta, even though there is no record in human or alien history of Ireta's previous exploration. The sudden mutiny of the heavy-worlders seems a bit of a mystery; what motivates them? Is it the equally mysterious rumor that the exploratory team has been "planted"—abandoned to colonize Ireta without the team's prior knowledge or consent? The ending of the novel, too, is highly unresolved: unable to communicate with their parent ship, the survivors of the heavy-worlders' mutiny hope that their message has reached the friendly alien Tor. They embed their shuttle in an abandoned giff-cave and place themselves in suspended animation. The novel screams for a sequel.

The vegetarian ethic of the novel may leave some readers dissatisfied. Varian and Kai are repelled by the way the tyrannosaurus rex munches upon its victim instead of killing cleanly. Yet they seem nowhere near as concerned about whether the fish caught by the giffs are dealt clean deaths. The Galormi, a carnivorous race that feeds upon prey paralyzed with venom, are regarded as the eiptome of evil, not simply as animals following instinct. Varian seems unconcerned that her civilization has deliberately exterminated them. And the violence and evil of the heavy-worlders seem to grow out of their meat-eating, a bloodlust that is sexual and hysterical. McCaffrey herself is active in protecting animals from mistreatment, but I wonder if the reader is expected to accept the vegetarian bias of the novel unquestioningly.

Stylistically and thematically, the novel is worth reading in spite of its lack of resolution. The blandness of the hero and heroine is curiously at odds with the highly technical vocabulary. McCaffrey might lose the amateur in her casual allusions to matters of stellar evolution and current theories of warm-blooded dinosaurs. And there is probably symbolic significance in the fact that, on a world of warm-blooded dinosaurs, Kai and Varian swallow a drug to make them cold-blooded, while they sleep out the time until their rescue.

Though McCaffrey takes pains to develop worlds with different value systems, certain leitmotiffs reappear from her other work. Interest in and accurate portrayal of children are positive features of this novel, as with many others. The fact that Varian discovers a cave containing an egg from an intelligent avian and then later takes refuge in that same cave is a surprising echo of Menolly's experience in *Dragonsong*. One passage in *Dinosaur Planet* demonstrates that the resemblance is not accidental: Varian and Kai discuss the fascination of flight and the dream of being an avian creature, "to dip, dive, soar, and glide" (*DP* 110). They agree that this yearning toward the freedom of flight is a universal human longing. Giffs are another winged species in McCaffrey's works, an echo of McCaffrey's fire lizards, dragons, and pervasive horse-and-rider motif.

The existence of Dandy, the baby hyracotherium, also reminds us of McCaffrey's love of horses, expecially since she uses Dandy to direct reader sympathy: initially by associating him with the children, and later by showing that the brutal heavy-worlders have callously killed him.

Many of the puzzles of *Dinosaur Planet* are resolved in the last pages of *Dinosaur Planet Survivors*. Varian, Kai, and ten others are awakened after forty-three years of cold sleep. Although the action of *Survivors* is swift-paced, aspects of character and environment go unexplored. Varian's attraction for Aygar and her cooling passion for Kai seem unresolved. Though an explanation of Ireta's mixed ecology is given, the giffs remain a curiosity. It is not clear whether there will be a sequel. Ireta, the planet of dinosaurs, is not fully explored!

"The Greatest Love" (1977) has as its premise the idea that a woman who is unable to carry a child to full term because of a uterine abnormality is able to donate a fertilized ovum, which is then implanted in another woman's womb where it grows to term and results in a healthy baby, genetically the child of the woman with the abnormal womb. McCaffrey did extensive and meticulous research on this topic. Details concerning animal exogenesis, human reproductive anatomy, blood-typing, and even the theological and legal repercussions of this procedure are explained with economy and thoroughness in the novella. The plot involves an infertile woman, her husband, and her sister-in-law, the last of whom offers to be the host-mother. The complication of the story, however, is not the medical procedure, though this is explained convincingly. The complication revolves around the infertile woman's mother, Louise Baxter (whose name irresistibly echoes *louse* and *bastard*), whose neurotic narcissism prompts her to denounce the man and his sister as incestuous. The courtroom scene, in which these charges are disproved and Louise Baxter discredited, is a tour de force.

McCaffrey had experimented with the premise of implanting fertilized ova in host-mothers' wombs in her very first published story, "Freedom of the Race" (1953). However, the 1977 novella is, as might be expected, better researched, marked by more intricate characterization, and more elaborately plotted. Like many science-fiction writers of our time, McCaffrey explores reproductive technology and variation in many of her stories. In this particular case, however, she was something of a prophet, for the story was published only a year before the birth of Louise Brown, a baby who was the result of fertilization in a petri dish, with the resultant fertilized ovum being reimplanted in the mother's womb. Obviously, this is not the same procedure described in "The Greatest Love" since fertilization took place outside the mother's body and no third-party host-mother was involved. But it did involve the transplantation of a fertilized ovum into a human uterus, just as in McCaffrey's story.

Typical McCaffrey themes and devices are apparent in this novella. It is a feminist piece, because the maverick doctor who designs and performs the procedure is a woman, Allison Craft. Her first name is the same as that medieval feminist who gives such a stirring defense of both sexual congress and letting women have their own way: The Wife of Bath. The women in the story all show initiative and courage in obtaining their goals, and the two major men, Peter Kellogg, the prospective father, and Chuck Henderson, the physician who assists Allison Craft, are both shown as sympathetic and supportive. In fact, almost all the male characters show laudable understanding of the women's goals and aspirations. While Allison Craft excels in a male-dominated field, the genetic mother and the host-mother, Cecily and Pat Kellogg, both show their initiative in fulfilling traditional roles—in untraditional ways.

It is unusual for a McCaffrey story to use religious imagery or themes, but McCaffrey explores the theological implications of exogenesis. She uses a Catholic priest and a Presbyterian minister as spokesmen. The Protestant is not offended by the implications of virgin birth; for Pat, the host-mother, is a virgin during the whole process. The priest's opinion is never fully revealed. At least twice within the story, the Gospel according to John is alluded to: "Greater love has no man than this, that a man lay down his life for his friends" (John 15:13; "GL" 33, 44). However, McCaffrey gently turns this quotation to the title idea of the greatest love of all: not giving up life, but providing new life. These two uses of religious allusion are feminist in their reference to the importance of virgin birth in Christianity and the high value of giving life; their feminist impact is increased by the date on which Pat Kellogg gives birth: August 15, the date of the Immaculate Conception of the Blessed Virgin, the date on which Roman Catholics celebrate the uniqueness of a woman, the one human being in history conceived without the stain of original sin.

As a humorous footnote to our discussion of this novella, it might be noted that McCaffrey's favorite dog, Wizard, appears in this novella as he does in "The Great Canine Chorus" (see *GOTU*, 153–154).

The Coelura (1983) is a short novel based on the premise of cloth woven from a kind of animate thread, spun by a nearly extinct creature of the planet Demeathorn. The intricate social structure of the Federated Sentient Planets of the twenty-second century, based as it is on ostentation and passage of wealth from parent to heir-elect, endangers the coelura because of the greed of such as Lady Cinna, whose daughter Caissa vows to protect the lovely rainbow spinners. Caissa becomes involved in a romance with a mysterious stranger who turns out to be an heir to the coelura's habitat. She thus obtains a gown of precious coelura-woven fabric, the approval of her father, the protection of the coelura, and her own true love.

The Coelura uses themes and motifs McCaffrey has introduced elsewhere. There is the Atalanta theme, where the woman agrees to marry a man only if he will perform some monumental deed. This applies not to the heroine, Caissa, but to her mother Cinna, who has settled a contract with Caissa's father to bear his heir (Caissa) only if he promises to give her a dress of coelura. We saw the Atalanta theme in connection with Helva choosing her brawn and with queen dragons attempting to outfly their bronze suitors.

Another McCaffrey theme in the novel is the Cinderella motif. Caissa is not a wretched drudge at the beginning of the novel, true, but she is confined to a backwater planet. Lady Cinna, though her natural mother, behaves more like a wicked stepmother. Murrell, the Cavernus with whom Caissa signs an heir-contract (her equivalent to getting married), is a Prince Charming, though he also has elements of a frog-prince, deformed and abandoned as he is when she first sees him in a pool of water. Caissa's new gown, of coelura, is like the magical clothes bestowed on Cinderella, making Caissa one of many McCaffrey heroines who obtain beautiful new raiment. And the first time we see Caissa she is, like Cinderella, fleeing from the ball at midnight, barefoot.

As in other McCaffrey stories, there are touches of Shakespearean imagery, though too complex for discussion here. The isolation of Baythan and his daughter Caissa on a backwater planet with rainbow creatures who spin magic reminds us of *The Tempest,* with Baythan as Prospero, Caissa as Miranda, and the coelura as Ariel. The language, manners, and some of the names in the novel remind us of *Julius Caesar. Cinna,* for example, is the name of the conspirator who first strikes Caesar. Caissa's name sounds like Cassius, and other names are latinate in form and endings.

There is also a version of the horse-and-rider motif here, though much disguised and changed. The coelura spin cloth that reflects human emotion. They are rare and endangered, but beautiful. The cloth forms a symbiosis with the wearer, much like the symbiosis between dragon and rider. In effect, coelura represent the human imagination in much the same way the dragon, spaceship, pegasus, horse, and unicorn do in other McCaffrey fiction.

The Coelura is based on several innovative premises that could bear further development. Though the diction and manners of the characters are at times almost stilted, the themes do have appeal. The novel is almost fantasy rather than science fiction, lacking the thorough scientific background of *Dinosaur Planet* or "The Greatest Love." Stylistic elements make it more akin to early McCaffrey fiction. It lacks the power of McCaffrey's other recent work, but it still has originality and charm.

At least seven of McCaffrey's short stories have not been reprinted after their first appearance in magazines or anthologies. These are "Freedom of the Race" (1953), already discussed in chapter I; "Sittik" (1970); "Velvet Fields" (1973); "The Rescued Girls of Refugee" (1973); "Rabble-Dowser" (1973); "Cinderella Switch" (1980); and "Lady in Waiting" (1978). Two stories, "Habit Is an Old Horse" and "The Bones Do Lie," have been accepted but at this writing have not appeared in print. "The Bones Do Lie" is scheduled for appearance in Harlan Ellison's forthcoming *The Last Dangerous Visions,* to be published by Houghton-Mifflin. Ellison, in a letter dated November 27, 1983, describes it as a probable award winner, representing new heights in the quality of McCaffrey's work and having potential for expansion into a novel.

Two early McCaffrey stories, "Sittik" and "Velvet Fields," are essentially horror stories, with pessimistic endings quite out of character for McCaffrey. "Sittik" is an economically told story of a young boy who becomes depressed and finally dies because schoolmates call him a nonsensical word: "sittick." After his death, the name-callers begin to work on his mother. The story could be seen as a parable of intolerance; *sittik* has the same number of letters and phonemic configuration as *nigger* and could stand for any ethnic epithet. But in a larger sense, "Sittik" is another affirmation of McCaffrey's belief in the power of imagination. In most of her fiction, belief, particularly on the part of children, leads to accomplishment. And so does it here, but with an ironically tragic result.

"Velvet Fields" is about a tragic mistake made by colonists from Earth of the planet Zobranoirundisi. Believing the planet to be mysteriously abandoned, like the *Marie Celeste,* they graze their cattle on the beautiful green velvet fields. Too late, they realize that the peculiar life cycle of the indigenous sentient life has been interrupted by this grazing and that in essence the colonists have been eating the natives. The natives, as they are reborn, demand their flesh back, with the result that the colonists have to sacrifice various body parts, including the narrator's tongue. This rather grisly tale invokes the notion of original sin in an existentialist manner: the colonists regard the planet as an Eden, from which the original inhabitants may have been expelled for eating an apple.[1] But they retain an uneasy sense of being trespassers—and we sometimes use the word *trespass* for *sin.* It is in fact they, the colonists, who have transgressed by eating of the fruit. There is even a Tree of Life, one of the stages in the life cycle of the Zobranoirundisians. The name of the planet itself is apparently derived from the slavic root *sobrany,* meaning group or society, implying that the planet already has "society" or civilization. McCaffrey reinforces this interpretation of the story of original sin by having the ecologist, Martin Chavez, quote the sentence God put upon Adam and Eve when expelling them from Eden: "From dust ye came, to dust ye shall return, and from dust shall ye spring again" (Gen. 3:19).

McCaffrey apparently researched the ecology of her created planet very carefully—the story bristles with botanical terms. But it is unusual in her canon for its pessimism. The colonists are guilty only in ignorance; yet the implication is that such guilt might extend to any human being. The tragedy of the Siwannah in *Decision at Doona* does not have the same pessimism, for the Siwannah deliberately and stupidly committed mass suicide because of a human mistake. "Velvet Fields" is truly an existential interpretation of original sin: by the mere act of existing, taking sustenance, and feeding our young, we violate nature, even on Earth. How much more we might do so in an alien environment!

"The Rescued Girls of Refugee" shares a myth-like quality with "Sittik" and "Velvet Fields," but it is a story that affirms rather than denies human spirit. As on the planet Chloe in *The Ship Who Sang,* a repressive all-female society rules on Refugee. But then males come and telepathically broadcast dreams conditioning the younger women to join them in liberation and love. Each woman, in her dream, selects a partner from the men in the rescue ship. The long dream-sequence reported by the point-of-view character, Bannay, has an almost hallucinatory beauty. Bannay herself has elements of the Cinderella figure we see elsewhere in McCaffrey's fiction: the Wise Woman is a type of wicked stepmother, denying growth, pleasure, and romance. The brown-eyed knitting woman is the Fairy Godmother. Verden, of course, is the Prince, come to take Bannay away and endow her with riches and treasures in the magic carriage of the ship.

In sharp contrast to these stories of voodoo, Eden, and dreams is a witty, topical story called "Rabble-Dowser." Since the hero is a college president trying to prevent campus rioting, the story might well have conservative political implications, but in fact it is a rather knowledgeable treatment of campus politics in the late 1960s and early 1970s, examining many issues, such as campus building programs, minority hiring, and the Kent State May 4 deaths. One character, Stefan Lenczi, is the focus of dissent because he stubbornly maintains that no "ethnically pure black" has ever been a mathematician (a nonverifiable statement because it is difficult to prove that *any* black is "ethnically pure"). Lenczi seems a caricature of Arthur Jensen, who in real life made parallel assertions about ethnicity and intellectual potential.

The college president in the story, William Barry Rentnor, is approached by Dr. Berstock, who claims to be able to prevent riots with the help of an idiot empath named Jeremy Goslin. The character of Goslin seems very similar to Harold Orley in *To Ride Pegasus,* except that Goslin is a broadcast empath as well. Both are big and dangerous when roused; both are described as "human barometers." Actually, Berstock *causes* riots by unleashing Goslin on campus crowds. At the end, after Berstock has incited a crowd to tear down the math building, Rentnor is unable to revenge himself on Berstock and so resorts to petty expulsions and suspensions. However, he quietly follows student advice on the most important issue of student dissent, a subterranean building program. The characterizations and treatment of issues are light and deft, from the obnoxious, garlic-scented Lenczi to the diabolic Berstock who reminds the reader of other Svengali-like characters in McCaffrey's work: Monsorlit in *Restoree* and Lanzecki in *The Crystal Singer.*

"Cinderella Switch" is a light-hearted futuristic treatment of the Cinderella story but with the heroine far from the woebegone, helpless lass of the traditional story. Her identity, as she captivates three young men of the far-distant future, is a teasingly kept secret. McCaffrey enjoys describing exotic raiment, as in *The Coelura,* and outdoes herself in this story, where a mist of light shimmers around the heroine, concealing all but her eyes and hair. In this case, however, the heroine is her own fairy godmother—she has engineered the gown herself and has a rather prosaic if prestigious career when she isn't bedazzling young men at the Touch-Down Ball. One of the young men at the ball is named Fenn, but since his sister's name is Marla, he clearly is not the Nick Fenn of "Daughter" in *Get Off the Unicorn.* However, he may be a distant descendant of the Fenn family.

"Lady in Waiting" is a fantasy story, rather than true science fiction. It centers around a chest in the storage room of a cottage that seems to grant wishes, even if, as in "The Monkey's Paw," the wish is granted at the expense of more humane considerations. The heroine, Amy, allows her daughters and another child to play with the contents of the chest—but somehow they find ornate costumes instead of mundane sheets and cast-offs. Amy begins to suspect that the chest fulfills her need—even to the point of having caused her husband's death, thereby providing the insurance money to buy the cottage outright.

Again, there is the use of elaborate costume, magically produced, as with Cinderella. Again, the heroine is magically provided with wealth—although by her Prince being taken away rather than personally providing the wealth. A macabre touch is suggested when Amy, suspecting that the chest grants wishes, begins to formulate a wish that her husband return from the dead. She then smells a sweetish odor like that she smelled at her husband's funeral and recoils from the chest in horror—feeling, perhaps, that inside, this time, she will find not fancy costumes for little girls, but her husband's corpse. If the chest is a kind of fairy godmother, it is a malevolent fairy, granting wishes both innocent and evil.

In addition to the Cinderella theme, with the complex evil twist, there is also the typical McCaffrey affirmation of the power of the human imagination. It is clear that the chest is nothing more than a mirror of human desire, whether a little girl's desire to please her playmates with gauze and velvet gowns, a family's desire for self-sufficiency, or a widow's desire to undo her husband's death. Though the story is a sad one, the heroine comes to terms with the power of the chest—that is, the power of human imagination—by being able, in the final lines of the story, to bid it courteously goodnight, as if it were only human.

McCaffrey's three non-science-fiction novels—*The Mark of Merlin* (1971), *Ring of Fear* (1971), and *The Kilternan Legacy* (1975)—are sometimes described as gothics or romances, but they are not so easily classified. The first two are mysteries because, although they take a feminine point of view with romance interest, the plot of each centers around a crime and the discovery of its perpetrator. Beyond mere genre, these novels explore many of the images and themes that appear in McCaffrey's science fiction.

The Mark of Merlin, for example, does tell the romance of Carla Murdock and Major Regan Laird. But, from the moment the twenty-year-old Carla is committed to the custody of Laird as his legal ward, the two of them are intent on discovering who has murdered Carla's father. McCaffrey, ever the careful researcher, turns her talents to research on rare stamps and the lore of World War II. Herself the daughter of a military man, McCaffrey makes her heroine an "army brat." Skillful use of suspense, foreshadowing, and surprise create an entertaining plot for the novel. For a time, even Laird, with whom Carla has begun to fall in love, is a suspect in the killing, which has been motivated by looting of French national art treasures.

Characterization is far from the insipid formulaic stereotypes of the bad gothic romance. Carla, like most McCaffrey heroines, is far from helpless and ignorant of the world. Though she does fall into the arms of her soldier lover on a few occasions of helplessness, she is intelligent and resourceful, and she swears and drinks like a good little soldier herself. Merlin, her beautiful German shepherd, is a well-drawn character in the novel. McCaffrey really owned a German shepherd named Merlin, the son of Wizard who appears in "The Great Canine Chorus" and "The Greatest Love."

Several themes from McCaffrey's science fiction make an appearance in *The Mark of Merlin.* Carla is a Cinderella figure, though in the second chapter, she actually refers to herself as "no Cinderella" because of her recent illness. Merlin, with his magical name, is a male version of the fairy godmother. Carla's mother, a run-about who was probably killed on her way to meet an illicit lover, was cold and distant to her daughter—a wicked stepmother. Like so many of McCaffrey's Cinderella figures who echo the fairy tale of a girl losing her shoe while fleeing from the ball, Carla takes off her footwear and begins running barefoot only fifteen pages into the novel. The wintry setting admits of no transformation into glamourous ball-gowns, but when Carla and Laird recognize their mutual attraction, she suddenly stops wearing drab trousers and sweaters and changes to a red sweater and plaid skirt.

Laird also echoes a McCaffrey theme, mutilation. Like Harlan in *Restoree,* he combines the stories of the Frog Prince and the Ugly Duckling, having received disfiguring facial wounds, which, however, do not prevent Carla from finding him attractive. Her first kiss transfigures him, if not in reality, at least in his own eyes. Doctors at Walter Reed Hospital will do the rest. The other ugly duckling in the story is Turtle Bailey, who was beaten by boys envious of his beautiful voice. No such transformation exists for Turtle, however; though his mutilation, like Menolly's in *Dragonsong*, deprives him of music, there is no restoration, only bleak tragedy.

Ring of Fear, while it has a romance interest, adheres even less to the romance formula than *The Mark of Merlin*. As well as being a mystery, it contains a number of explicit sex scenes. Briefly, it is the story of Nialla Donnelly, whose father has been murdered and who has been raped. She meets Rafe Clery, a millionaire who has fallen in love with her from earlier meetings. He is able to dispel her rape-traumatized revulsion for the sex act; the two marry and solve the mystery of her father's death.

This brief summary fails to convey the intricacy of the plot; the symbolism of the story likewise shows complexity. Nialla is a Cinderella figure, most obviously; she goes from rags to riches, gets beautiful new clothes, and runs barefoot in moments of crisis, like many of McCaffrey's Cinderellas. The horse-and-rider motif is invoked throughout the novel because Rafe and Nialla are committed to a life of breeding, training, and showing horses. In fact, the scenes of horses riding and jumping are instructive in understanding scenes of dragon-riding in the Pern novels, both in terms of the experience of riding and its significance for the rider.

McCaffrey also selects names from Hindu, Roman, and Christian mythology to enrich the central plot of the love relationship. One of Nialla's horses, known in show circuits for his vicious temper, is called Juggernaut. Juggernaut, or Jagannath, is the name of an incarnation of Vishnu, best known among Westerners for the tradition that his worshippers are sometimes crushed under the wheels of his huge chariot. The black face of representations of Jagannath is reflected in the horse's black coat. The horse Juggernaut's disposition, however, has been the result of mistreatment planned to make him spirited. Through kindness, and through the friendship of her Maine coon cat, Nialla is able to tame Juggernaut. Since he has been through hell, she renames him Orfeo, and the cat (though it is male) is Eurydice. The spelling of *Orfeo* suggests the Gluck opera, *Orfeo ed Eurydice*, probably because the opera ends happily, whereas the Roman myth does not. In the opera, Orfeo is told he may lead his wife Eurydice back from Hades if he can avoid looking at her. Finally, at her entreaties, he loses his resolve and does look at her, whereupon she dies. However, Amor restores her to life, feeling that Orfeo has been tried sufficiently.

Nialla, too, has been through a living hell as a result of her father's murder and her own rape, so that her story parallels Orfeo's, her horse's. She is rescued by the love of Rafe, whose real name is Rafael. This is a form of *Raphael*, meaning healer, and the name evokes the story of Tobias and Sara, Biblical lovers whose story is told in the Book of Tobias. Tobias's father has been blinded; he has been sent to collect a debt. He meets Sara, who has been betrothed seven times, although a demon has killed each husband. The Lord sends the angel Raphael to cure the father's blindness and to help them; through Raphael's advice and aid, the two are able to marry without Tobias's falling prey to the demon. The story parallels Nialla's, since she has been effectively prevented from fulfilling her sexual potential by a "demon" of rape. Though Rafe has a checkered past, he performs the role of healer with Nialla and casts out her "demon."

The Kilternan Legacy is not a crime mystery, though it contains an apparent murder, a shadowy private detective, and a man with an enigmatic past. It is the nearest of any of these non-science-fiction novels to being a romance, but if it is one, it is a very sophisticated romance. The heroine, Irene Teasey, is a thirty-six-year-old divorcee who has inherited a small country estate in Ireland from an aunt she has never met. The real "mystery" of the book involves Irene's perception of her aunt, whom she will never know, but whose personality gradually becomes as clear as any in the book. The "mysterious legacy" plot device is common in gothic romances, but McCaffrey's treatment of it is far richer and more literary than, for example, a Harlequin Romance with a similar premise, such as Victoria Woolf's *Sweet Compulsion* (Stratford, Ontario, Canada: Harlequin, 1979). Though there may be superficial similarities, McCaffrey's characterization is much deeper, and McCaffrey uses complex imagery.

Though space limitations prevent extended analysis, it is apparent from some of the personal names in the novel and from Kieron's chess set, in which each piece represents a character from Irish legends, that McCaffrey is using imagery from Celtic myth to embellish and enrich this tale. The particular Gilbert and Sullivan songs alluded to in the novel also have significance. Horses appear in this novel, too; again, with Snow's infatuation with Horseface (this was also McCaffrey's nickname for one of her own real-life horses), the primacy of imagination is invoked, for it is the love of horses that makes Snow plead with her mother to allow vision to rule over mundane, plodding routine, so that the family can live in Ireland rather than return to their repressed, unimaginative existence in the United States. There is a parallel between Snow's love of the horse, her twin brother Simon's love of motorcycles, and Irene's own delight in the beautiful Mercedes she has inherited from her aunt. All are versions of the horse-and-rider motif—the triumph of imagination, as represented by a beautiful horse or vehicle.

The image of a disabled artist is invoked again, as it was with Menolly's wounded hand in *Dragonsong* and or Turtle's battered vocal chords in *The Mark of Merlin* because Irene learns that her dead aunt was forced to stop singing professionally when, during a World War II bombing, her vocal chords were pierced by splinters of glass. The aunt's case is less tragic, however, since she has already had her singing career.

Finally, the novel has distinct feminist implications, particularly in the portrait of Irene Teasey learning independence after a degrading marriage, in the unpleasant portrayal of her male-chauvinist ex-husband Teddie, and in Kieron Thornton's colloquy on Irish marriage and divorce.

Alchemy and Academe (1970) is a collection of short stories by sundry hands, edited by McCaffrey. The theme, as explained with considerable word-play in McCaffrey's introduction, was conceived while McCaffrey was discussing a story with Sonya Dorman. The idea is that *alchemy* (changes in the fundamental nature of things) could be similar to *academe* (which promotes changes in the fundamental nature of minds). The anthology includes fifteen stories written expressly for the collection, two reprinted stories, and three poems. Poetry is unusual in a science fiction anthology, and what is more unusual is that McCaffrey's brief head-notes are also in several cases poetry—some quoted, some her own. Interestingly, the story of Peter Tate, "Mainchance," about the evolution of intelligence, quotes the portion of Pope's *An Essay on Man* that McCaffrey used in *To Ride Pegasus* to illumine humankind's "middle state."

In addition to being a very poetic anthology for science fiction, the collection also contains a great deal of wit and humor, starting with McCaffrey's own "Foreword" and continuing with such stories as James Blish's "More Light," a parody of Robert W. Chambers's *The King in Yellow*.

Even in writing a cookbook, McCaffrey does not turn hack. *Cooking Out of this World* (1973) is a compilation of recipes by sixty-two science-fiction writers. Some, like the eleven contributed by McCaffrey herself, are quite usable recipes, though research for this volume did not include kitchen-testing all of them. McCaffrey's quiche, which I have sampled but which is not in the book, suggests that she is a trustworthy source of culinary advice. Others, such as John Sladek's Fountain Pen Stew, are usable in spite of their risable presentation. Some, however, such as David Gerrold's Serendipity Curry or Avram Davidson's Old Prospector's Style Coffee, are clearly not meant to be taken seriously. My favorite, Gopher Stew, by Walter M. Miller, Jr., includes directions for avoiding being bitten by a diamondback rattler and overcoming the revulsion and guilt involved in shooting the gopher, which even after death is "very persistent" (*COW* 138).

The recipes were provided to McCaffrey especially for this book and illustrate two principles of McCaffrey's thought that apply to her literary work: first, humor; second, the extent to which her work is grounded in the physical. No one (except Helva, and even Helva wants Niall to taste apples for her to experience secondhand) ever ignores food in a McCaffrey work. In fact, throughout most of her work, everything of importance happens at breakfast, lunch, or dinner. Even alien meals are described in imaginative detail.

Cooking Out of this World is at the present writing almost a rare book. There is some discussion of reprinting it. Collectors of McCaffrey, of science fiction in general, and of odd literary cookbooks have made it a scarce item.

To end a book about McCaffrey's work with discussion of a cookbook may seem trivial; however, it exemplifies the scope of her work. Her early work includes a parody of a gothic-romance-space-opera; she has written very hard science fiction with elaborately worked-out ecologies and science fiction so soft it has won a Gandalf for book-length fantasy (*The White Dragon*); she has written murder mysteries, literary essays, and a romance; she has edited an anthology and created a cookbook. She has even had another artistic career—in music and theater—and simply appropriated the knowledge from that field for use in her writing. Her imagery is drawn from the languages and legends of many countries, from Shakespeare and from musical comedy. She has created the notion of an imaginary animal so detailed that she can describe its anatomy well enough to create a scene where surgery is being performed on it (in *Moreta, Dragonlady of Pern*). Though her most pervasive theme is the power of the imagination, her descriptions of setting and action include the most concrete of details: food, animal behavior, clothing, even outhouses. Her primary image, that of a horse and a rider, which represents the imagination and the talented individual, is presented in so many guises—from spaceship and cyborg, dragon and rider, pegasus and talent, unicorn and maiden—that each new representation illuminates new facets of the human imagination.

Though sometimes criticized for sentimentality, she has created portraits of admirable, feminist women, realistic children, and fascinating, believable men. But above any particular element, praise must be given to the inventive fun and joy in her work. She is a writer with an unconquerable sense that the universe is a place where man and woman may seek to wonder, to enjoy, to explore, to procreate, to doubt perhaps, but ultimately to know; to die perhaps, but to know love; to age and forget, but to give birth and propel their children into the wonderful future, into the marvelous universe, mounted on steeds of pure joy, born on the backs of imagination.

NOTE

[1] *If,* 22, no. 2 (November/December 1973), p. 92.

VIII
BIBLIOGRAPHY OF FIRST EDITIONS OF FICTION
AND SELECTED NON-FICTION BY McCAFFREY

This is a list of McCaffrey's fiction. I have arbitrarily included selected interviews under secondary works. More exhaustive bibliographical information can be found in Rosemarie Arbur's *Leigh Brackett, Marion Zimmer Bradley, Anne McCaffrey: A Primary and Secondary Bibliography*, Boston: G. K. Hall, 1982, and in Lloyd Currey's *Science Fiction and Fantasy Authors: A Bibliography of First Printings of Their Fiction*, Boston: G. K. Hall, 1979, pp. 339–340.

Alchemy and Academe. Garden City: Doubleday, 1970. McCaffrey edited this story collection and wrote the foreword.

"Apple." In *Crime Prevention in the 30th Century.* Ed. Hans Stefan Santesson. New York: Walker, 1969, pp. 89–115. Also in *To Ride Pegasus* and *Get Off the Unicorn.*

"A Bridle for Pegasus." *Analog,* July 1973, pp. 10–70. Also in *To Ride Pegasus.*

"A Change of Hobbit." *Ireland of the Welcomes,* 26, No. 4 (July/August 1977), 34–35.

"Changeling." In *Get Off the Unicorn.* New York: Ballantine, 1977, pp. 99–116.

"Cinderella Switch." In *Stellar #6: Science Fiction Stories.* Ed. Judy-Lynn del Rey. New York: Ballantine/Del Rey, 1981, pp. 110–121.

The Coelura. San Francisco: Underwood-Miller, 1983.

Cooking Out of This World [cookbook]. New York: Ballantine, 1973.

The Crystal Singer. London: Severn House, 1982. Also published as *Crystal Singer,* Garden City, New York: Doubleday; and New York: Ballantine/Del Rey. There are significant differences between British and American editions.

"Daughter." In *The Many Worlds of Science Fiction.* Ed. Ben Bova. New York: E. P. Dutton, 1971, pp. 139–165. Also in *Get Off the Unicorn.*

Decision at Doona. New York: Ballantine, 1969.

Dinosaur Planet. London: Futura, 1978.

Dinosaur Planet Survivors. London: Futura, 1984.

"The Dragon Series." In *The Great Science Fiction Series.* Ed. Frederik Pohl. New York: Harper & Row, 1980, pp. 259–261.

Dragondrums. New York: Atheneum, 1979.

Dragonflight. New York: Ballantine, 1968.

Dragonquest. New York: Ballantine, 1971.

"Dragonrider." Part One: *Analog,* December 1967, pp. 8–61. Part Two: *Analog,* January 1968, pp. 112–163.

The Dragonriders of Pern. Garden City: Nelson Doubleday [Science Fiction Book Club], 1978. Omnibus edition of *Dragonflight, Dragonquest,* and *The White Dragon.*

Dragonsinger. New York: Atheneum, 1977.

Dragonsong. New York: Atheneum; London: Sidgwick & Jackson, 1976.

"Dramatic Mission." *Analog,* June 1969, pp. 48–99. Revised in *The Ship Who Sang.*

"Dull Drums." In *Future Quest.* Ed. Roger Elwood. New York: Avon, 1973, pp. 11–34. Also in *Get Off the Unicorn.*

"Finders Keepers" [McCaffrey's title: "Finder's Keeper"]. *The Haunt of Horror,* 1, No. 2 (August 1973), 95–104. Also in *Get Off the Unicorn.*

"Freedom of the Race." *Science-Fiction Plus,* 1, No. 6 (October 1953), p. 20.

Get Off the Unicorn. New York: Ballantine, 1977. Includes: "Lady in the Tower," "A Meeting of the Minds," "Daughter," "Dull Drums," "Changeling," "Weather on Welladay," "The Thorns of Barevi," "Horse from a Different Sea," "The Great Canine Chorus," "Finder's Keeper," "A Proper Santa Claus," "The Smallest Dragonboy," "Apple," and "Honeymoon."

"The Great Canine Chorus." In *Infinity One.* Ed. Robert Hoskins. New York: Lancer, 1970, pp. 67–84. Also in *Get Off the Unicorn.*

"The Greatest Love." In *Futurelove.* Ed. Roger Elwood. Indianapolis: Bobbs-Merrill, 1977, pp. 1–71.

"The Helva Series." In *The Great Science Fiction Series.* Ed. Frederik Pohl. New York, Harper & Row, 1980, p. 273.

"Hitch Your Dragon to a Star: Romance and Glamour in Science Fiction." In *Science Fiction, Today, and Tomorrow.* Ed. Reginald Bretnor. New York: Harper & Row, 1974, pp. 278–292.

"Honeymoon." In *Get Off the Unicorn.* New York: Ballantine, 1977, pp. 266–303.

"Killashandra—Coda and Finale." In *Continuum 4.* Ed. Roger Elwood. New York: G. P. Putnam's Sons, 1975, pp. 108–142.

"Killashandra—Crystal Singer." In *Continuum 2.* Ed. Roger Elwood. New York: G. P. Putnam's Sons, 1974, pp. 138–180.

The Kilternan Legacy. New York: Dell, 1975. I have seen only the later Millington edition.

"The Lady in the Tower." *F&SF,* April 1959, pp. 62–79. Also in *Get Off the Unicorn,* 1977.

"Lady in Waiting." In *Cassandra Rising.* Ed. Alice Laurence. Garden City: Doubleday, 1978, pp. 89–100.

The Mark of Merlin. New York: Dell, 1971. I have seen only the later Millington edition.

"A Meeting of Minds." *F&SF,* January 1969, pp. 5–33.

"Milekey Mountain." In *Continuum 3.* Ed. Roger Elwood. New York: G. P. Putnam's Sons, 1974, pp. 111–136.

Moreta: Dragonlady of Pern. New York: Ballantine/Del Rey, 1983.

"My Bold Irish Lad." *Ireland of the Welcomes,* 27, No. 6 (November/ December 1978), 16-17.

"On Pernography." *Algol,* No. 14 (Fall 1968), pp. 16-17.

"Prelude to a Crystal Song." In *Continuum 1.* Ed. Roger Elwood. New York: G. P. Putnam's Sons, 1974, pp. 123-157.

"A Proper Santa Claus." In *Demon Kind.* Ed. Roger Elwood. New York: Avon, 1973, pp. 100-109. Xerox provided by David Aylward of Spaced Out Library. Also in *Get Off the Unicorn.*

"Rabble-Dowser." In *Omega.* Ed. Roger Elwood. New York: Walker, 1973, pp. 113-133.

"Randall Garrett." In *The Best of Randall Garrett.* Ed. Robert Silverberg. New York: Pocket, 1982, pp. 165-167.

"The Rescued Girls of Refugee." In *Ten Tomorrows.* Ed. Roger Elwood. Greenwich, Conn.: Fawcett, 1973, pp. 67-74.

Restoree. New York: Ballantine; London: Rapp & Whiting, 1967.

Ring of Fear. New York: Dell, 1971. I have seen only the later Millington edition.

"The Ship Who Disappeared." *Worlds of If,* 19, No. 3 (March 1969), 45-66. Later, revised, became "The Ship Who Dissembled," in *The Ship Who Sang.*

"The Ship Who Killed." *Galaxy,* October 1966, pp. 80-115. Later revised in *The Ship Who Sang.*

"The Ship Who Mourned." *Analog,* March 1966, pp. 41-60. Later revised in *The Ship Who Sang.*

"The Ship Who Sang," *F&SF,* April 1961, pp. 35-51. Later revised in *The Ship Who Sang.*

The Ship Who Sang. New York: Walker, 1969.

"Sittik." *Galaxy,* July 1970, pp. 99-101. (Title spelled incorrectly in magazine.)

"The Smallest Dragonboy." In *Science Fiction Tales.* Ed. Roger Elwood. Chicago: Rand McNally, 1973, pp. 15-32. Also in *Get Off the Unicorn.* Widely anthologized.

"The Thorns of Barevi." In *The Disappearing Future.* Ed. George Hay. London: Panther, 1970, pp. 35-44. Also in *Get Off the Unicorn,* 1977.

A Time When. Boston: NESFA Press, 1975. Revised in *The White Dragon.*

To Ride Pegasus. New York: Ballantine, 1973.

"The Unscientific Approach to Science Fiction: A Speech by Anne McCaffrey." *Luna',* No. 8 (1970), pp. 3-9.

"Velvet Fields." *Worlds of IF,* 22, No. 2 (November/December 1973), 91-98.

"Weather on Welladay." *Galaxy,* March 1969, pp. 77-111. Also in *Get Off the Unicorn,* 1977.

"Weyr Search." *Analog,* October 1967, pp. 8-60. Revised as opening of *Dragonflight.*

The White Dragon. New York: Ballantine, 1978.

"A Womanly Talent." *Analog,* February 1969, pp. 8-55. Also part of *To Ride Pegasus.*

IX

BIBLIOGRAPHY OF SELECTED SECONDARY WORKS

For a bibliography of 165 secondary items, see Arbur, below. Here I include a selection of works chosen for variety and critical significance, and in some cases because they postdate the Arbur volume.

Arbur, Rosemarie. *Leigh Brackett, Marion Zimmer Bradley, Anne McCaf-frey: A Primary and Secondary Bibliography*. Boston: G. K. Hall, 1982.
> Valuable both for ambitious bibliography and for evaluative essay, in spite of occasional typos. Indispensable for McCaffrey scholars.
Asimov, Isaac. *Asimov on Science Fiction*. Garden City, NY: Doubleday, 1981. P. 146.
> Discusses *The Ship Who Sang* in relation to other stories of cyborgs and of artificial intelligence.
Barr, Marleen. "Science Fiction and the Fact of Women's Repressed Crea-tivity: Anne McCaffrey Portrays a Female Artist." *Extrapolation*, 23, No. 1 (Spring 1982), 70–76.
> Feminist interpretation of character of Menolly. Refreshingly in-tellectual.
Biggle, Lloyd, Jr. *The Double: Bill Symposium*. Ed. Bill Mallardi and Bill Bowers. Akron, Ohio: D:B Press, 1969. Xerox provided by William Bowers.
> Answers to eleven questions about science fiction writing, answered by almost a hundred writers. McCaffrey's answers are hard to sum-marize, but show her brisk, unpretentious attitude toward her art.
Bleiler, E. F. *Science Fiction Writers: Critical Studies of the Major Authors from the Early Nineteenth Century to the Present Day*. New York: Charles Scribner's Sons, 1982. P. 3.
> Short mention, but important for categorizing the dragon novels "between legend, fairy tale, and science fiction."
Brizzi, Mary T. "McCaffrey, Anne (Inez)" [encyclopedia article]. In *Twentieth-Century Science-Fiction Writers*. Ed. Curtis C. Smith. New York: St. Martin's Press, 1981. P. 364.
> Praises McCaffrey's characterization and elaborate extrapolation upon scientific knowledge, mentioning that the latter has been underrated by critics.
"Narcissism and Romance in McCaffrey's *Restoree*." In *Patterns of the Fantastic*. Ed. Donald M. Hassler. Mercer Island, WA: Starmont House, 1983. Pp. 41–46.

Traces fairy-tale motifs and feminine erotic fantasies in *Restoree* through other McCaffrey works. My opinion has evolved since I wrote this article.

Crystal Singer (fanzine). Issues 1–10, 13–14 (c. 1978–79).
Newsletter devoted to the writings of Anne McCaffrey. Contains reviews, letters, art, notices, an occasional essay, etc. Apparently ceased publication with #14.

Ellison, Harlan. "A Voice from the Styx." In *The Book of Ellison.* Ed. Andrew Porter. New York: *Algol,* 1978. Pp. 127–140.
Detailed stylistic analysis; sharp insights into matters of diction. Some discussion of the issue of gender. Reprint of an earlier, difficult-to-obtain article (*Psychotic,* 27 (September 1968), 5–11).

Fonstad, Karen Wynn. *The Atlas of Pern.* New York: Ballantine, 1984.
Detailed maps, tables, floorplans, combat orchestrations, etc. based on the Pern novels and interviews. Some errors; disputable chronology. Authorized by McCaffrey, who adds prefatory letter.

Gordon, Andrew. "Human, More or Less: Man-Machine Communion in Samuel R. Delany's *Nova* and Other Science Fiction Stories." In *The Mechanical God, Machines in Science Fiction.* Ed. Thomas P. Dunn and Richard D. Erlich. Westport, Conn.: Greenwood Press, 1982. Pp. 193–202.
On pages 195 and 196 accuses McCaffrey of sentimentality in *The Ship Who Sang,* which he compares unfavorably with Frederik Pohl's *Man Plus.* Says she "bypasses . . . horrific aspects of cyborgization." Dislikes treatment of Niall's grotesque passion.

Harrison, M. John. "Absorbing the Miraculous." In *New Worlds #7.* Ed. Hilary Bailey and Charles Platt. London: Sphere, 1974. Pp. 205–207. American Edition: *New Worlds #6.* New York: Avon, 1975. Pp. 221–225.
Aggressive charge of elitism and intellectual/economic snobbery in *To Ride Pegasus.* Accuses McCaffrey of the "murder of Reason," "greasy sentiment," and "inexcusable prose."

Jonas, Gerald. "Imaginary People" (review of *Crystal Singer,* Ballantine paper edition). *New York Times Book Review,* 29 August 1982, p. 11.
Observes detailed world-sculpting, but fails to notice irony or symbolism.

Jones, Anne Hudson. "The Cyborg (R) Evolution in Science Fiction." In *The Mechanical God, Machines in Science Fiction.* Ed. Thomas P. Dunn and Richard D. Erlich. Westport, Conn.: Greenwood Press, 1982. Pp. 203–210.
Calls *The Ship Who Sang* an "anthology of stories," but praises the theme of humanizing the cyborg.

Katerinsky, Rhoda. "What to Read this Summer." *Ms.,* July 1979, p. 30.
Review of *The White Dragon.* Emphasizes political themes. Significant recognition in feminist periodical.

Knight, Damon. "What Is Science Fiction?" In *Turning Points: Essays on*

the Art of Science Fiction. Ed. Damon Knight.' New York: Harper &
Row, 1977. Pp. 62–69.

"Weyr Search" has five of the seven criteria cited in definitions of
science fiction. Hugo winners average 3.8; so McCaffrey is more
"science-fictional" than the average. Presented in tabular form; con-
clusions mine.

Landow, George P. "And the World Became Strange." In *The Aesthetics
of Fantasy Literature and Art.* Ed. Roger C. Schlobin. Notre Dame,
Indiana: University of Notre Dame Press, 1982. P. 131.

Calls McCaffrey a superior creator of fantasy, in company with
Ursula K. LeGuin and J. R. R. Tolkien.

Lundwall, Sam J. *Science Fiction: What It's All About.* New York: Ace,
1971. Pp. 143–144, 154, 165.

Short but significant commentary on "A Womanly Talent," and the
stories that later became *The Ship Who Sang.*

Mathews, Patricia. "Dragons and Daughters." *The Stone and the Stars,* 2,
No. 1 (March 1981), 9–11, 24.

Well-argued essay suggesting that McCaffrey's work, far from being
feminist, only depicts realistic family relationships in the harsh,
patriarchal mode—the talented daughter repressed by the domineer-
ing father. Address: Tess Kolney, Box 14259, Minneapolis, MN
55414.

Meyers, Walter E. *Aliens and Linguists: Language Study and Science Fiction.* Athen, GA: University of Georgia Press, 1980. P. 47.

This award-winning study mentions "The Ship Who Sang" to show
how the theme of depersonalization in connection with language
and machines is developed with cyborgs. Meyers also accuses McCaffrey of "nonsense" in describing Helva's vocal tricks, showing that
what makes sense to a trained vocalist may not make sense to a
linguist.

Morgan, Chris. "Science Fiction with Dragons . . . An Interview with Anne
McCaffrey." *Extro Science Fiction,* 1, No. 3, Whole number 75 (July/
August, 1982), 18–22. Appeared simultaneously as "Interview: Anne
McCaffrey." *Science Fiction Review,* 11, No. 3, Whole number 44
(August 1982), 20–24.

Reveals early influences, methods of research, sources, and plans for
further writing.

Naha, Ed. "Living with Dragons: Anne McCaffrey" (interview). *Future,*
No. 6 (November 1978), pp. 22–23, 74.

Interview. Many insights into McCaffrey's craft.

Pinder, Steve. "Dragondame: An Interview with Anne McCaffrey." *Fantasy Media,* 1, No. 2 (June/July 1979), 3–4.

Interview with McCaffrey. Insight into genesis of later Pern books
and McCaffrey's own evaluation of her later works.

Raymer, Anne Carolyn. *"The Ship Who Sang"* In *Survey of Science Fiction Literature.* Ed. Frank N. Magill. Englewood Cliffs: Salem Press,
1979. IV, 1917–1921.

Unusual approach; calls the book "Space Gothic," emphasizing "sinister imagery." Does not regard the book as an integrated novel.

Rutledge, Amelia A. "McCaffrey, Anne. *The Crystal Singer*" (review). *Science Fiction & Fantasy Book Review*, Issue 6 (July/August 1982), pp. 29–30.

Comments on the feminist themes in the book, but fails to recognize McCaffrey's ironic treatment of Killashandra's relationship with Lanzecki and the Guild.

Schwartz, Susan. "Women and Science Fiction." *New York Times Book Review*, 2 May 1982, pp. 11, 26–27.

McCaffrey cited as trail-blazer because of having the courage to publish under a feminine first name. Later, the article describes *why* this took courage.

Searles, Baird, Martin Last, Beth Meacham, and Michael Franklin. *A Reader's Guide to Science Fiction*. New York: Avon, 1979. Pp. 117–118.

Overview of McCaffrey's work up to 1979. Incorrectly identifies *The Ship Who Sang* as a "collection" and indicates that only Helva's *brain* is installed in her ship. Better on the Dragon series and *Dinosaur Planet*.

Warrick, Patricia S. *The Cybernetic Imagination in Science Fiction*. Cambridge, MA: MIT Press, 1980. P. 180.

Cites *The Ship Who Sang* for its optimistic portrayal of cyborgs.

Wolfe, Gary K. "The Encounter with Fantasy." In *The Aesthetics of Fantasy Literature and Art*. Ed. Roger C. Schlobin. Notre Dame, Indiana: University of Notre Dame Press, 1982. P. 7.

Relates Dragonriders books to sword-and-sorcery.

Wolfe, Gary K. *The Known and the Unknown: The Iconography of Science Fiction*. Kent, OH: Kent State University Press, 1979. Pp. 59, 78, 80–84.

Witty analysis, especially of Helva's relationship with Niall, but biassed toward Wolfe's general thesis that spaceships are cozy places.

Wolinsky, Richard, and Laurence Davidson. "Rigel Interviews Anne McCaffrey." *Rigel,* Issue 3 (Winter 1982), pp. 19–24.

Revealing on methods of composition, science research, and relationships with various editors.

Wood, Susan. "Women and Science Fiction." *Algol/Starship,* 16, No. 1, Whole Number 33 (Winter 1978–79), pp. 9–18.

Rebuttal of Sam Lundwall on "A Womanly Talent," on p. 11; other mentions of McCaffrey.

Wooster, Martin Morse. *"The White Dragon"* (review). *Science Fiction Review*, 8, No. 4, Whole number 32 (August 1979), p. 52.

The premise of rediscovered technology shows McCaffrey's antecedents in John Campbell, but the action is "Gothic." The series is worthy of a Hugo, but this book, while "a major novel," is "not brilliant."

Zeek, A. E., et al. *Pern Portfolio*. Staten Island, NY: Isis/Yggdrisil Press, 1978.

Art, poetry, fan fiction, and speculative essays on McCaffrey's work. Contains short essay on the genesis of dragons by McCaffrey herself. Essay by Deborah Burros discusses Pernese dragons and those of Ursula K. LeGuin in relation to dragons in Oriental and Western tradition. Address: Box 296, Staten Island, NY 10301.

INDEX